THINK YOUR WAY TO RICHES

Family Style

A Guide Book for the Family who Desires to:

- Release the "Natural Brilliance" within You and Your Children
- Help invent your Childs Personal "Model to Success"
- Discover Practical Methods to Create what you want for Yourself and Your Children
- Bring Back… Hope and Enthusiasm into your Family's Life

Written by Carrie Carter

FOREWORD BY TED CIUBA
THE NEW THINK AND GROW RICH AUTHOR

NEW YORK

Think Your Way To Riches
Family Style

ISBN: 978-1-60037-336-7 (Paperback)

Published by:

KNOWLEDGE EXCHANGE PRESS
An Imprint of Morgan James Publishing, LLC

Knowledge Exchange Press
1225 Franklin Ave Ste 325
Garden City, NY 11530-1693
Toll Free 800-485-4943
www.MorganJamesPublishing.com

Habitat for Humanity®
Peninsula
Building Partner

General Editor:
Heather Campbell

Cover Design by:
Vaughan Davison
www.KillerCovers.com

Orders & Enrollments:

810.714.3338

Think Your Way To Riches LLC
10520 Rustic Ridge
Fenton, Michigan 48430 USA

**Speeches, Workshops
and Consulting**

You can Book Carrie Carter
at your event! Contact Carrie
Carter at 810.714.3338

Interior Design by:
3 Dog Design
www.3dogdesign.net

Table of Contents

Acknowledgements

I would like to acknowledge YOU, the families who are taking the first step to create the lives you desire. It is not by CHANCE that you have this book. You have already taken the first step; you have applied the LAW of ATTRACTION to attract it to you. May you as a family learn and utilize the Universal Laws of Success to manifest the abundant lives of which you are worthy.

I would like to thank my mentor Ted Ciuba. Your master mind sessions and coaching gave me the passion to write my first book THINK YOUR WAY TO RICHES™ KIDS' STYLE.

You are truly an inspiration to me and the world. I feel blessed to be able to call you my friend.

I want to thank my sons Jeffrey Adams and Earl Carter along with my daughter-in-law Rachel, my soon to be daughter-in-law Jennifer, and my three granddaughters Kendall, Chloe, and Emily. My love for you has been instrumental in me writing this family book. You are all a blessing to me.

I want to thank my daughter Jennifer Lynn. Your birth, life, and death taught me so much about love, faith, and myself. I would not be the woman I am today had you not blessed me with being your mom. I love you.

I also want to acknowledge the beautiful children of the world. Though you are still young, you have the power to manifest the lives you desire. May you all learn the Universal Laws of Success and utilize them wisely. For you, little ones, hold the key to the future.

Blessings,

Carrie

Carrie Carter

Dedication

I dedicate this book to my husband Jim, whose faith in me to get my part of this book done amazed me.

Your patience, love, and desire to get this book out to the world, gave me the passion to write.

Foreword

Well-Being For The Whole Family

We live in a world of complexity, but this much is certain. If you are a parent or a child, your life, your responsibilities, and your joys include the whole family. Let's consider something that relates directly to the well-being of your children. Among scientists, scholars, and human potential leaders it's well accepted that we create our own worlds by the thoughts we entertain in our heads.

The thoughts we hold open us to vision, possibility, empowered action, and the working of the Law of Attraction, or mire us in a world of limitation, lack, anger, feeble or no purposeful action, and the working of the Law of Attraction. The Law of Cause and Effect operates throughout all levels of creation… in forward or reverse, it's the same Law.

In fact, there's a whole host of Universal seemingly secret Laws upon which the Universe runs.

You can learn how these laws work, and do amazing things… Like, isn't it amazing that though it took 100,000 years for humanity to figure out how to fly, once understanding came, humanity now uses those laws to reliably fly millions of passengers annually on intercontinental flights!??

A Distinct Difference

So why do most people live lives of lack and frustration, while others create lives of abundance and passion? It usually comes down to the people from whom they received their early (read unconsciously ingrained thoughts) training about how the world works around money. And since less than 5% of the population of even developed countries like the USA, Canada, or UK approach

Foreword

anything that could be remotely called financial abundance... Chances are you've been programmed by the 95% group!

So where is the point of intervention to creating that life of choice, contribution, and financial abundance? How do we move ourselves and our children from the competitive plane of existence to the creative plane? From the plane of limited options and limited resources, to a world of possibility, plenty, and choice?

Tool Your Thoughts

The answer is clearly, since we create our own worlds by the thoughts we encourage in our heads, you need to tool the thoughts you're encouraging in your head.

It's a matter of knowledge. Knowledge and Application.

It's a matter of first becoming aware of what we're doing, then working to understand and implement the Universal Laws of Success until they become instinctual and habitual.

If you're like most, you say, "Yeah, easier said than done."

Good news! Up steps one of the best positive-thinking books for the family that's ever been written!

The genius of Carrie Carter's rendition of the 12 Universal Laws of Success in *Think Your Way To Riches Family Style* is that she takes you leagues beyond the cerebral (which may not have any lasting effect) into processes and exercises the whole family participates in so all get it at the gut level.

Foreword

And when you get it there, you and all the family begin to live from that worldview. The quality of the results you create rises exponentially in every aspect of life!

Your children look up to you. You look to *Think Your Way To Riches Family Style* by Carrie Carter to guide your family to peace and abundance. Give your child the training you wish you could have had... Teach them... "You can be, do, and have any positive thing you want in this world by using the 12 secret Universal Laws of Success."

A leader in the human potential movement, Ted Ciuba - at www.Holo-Magic.com - writes and presents on harnessing that "HoloMagic c2 Factor" to acquire wealth and well-being. He presents a specific 13 point formula which works every time in his best-selling *The NEW Think and Grow Rich*. The book and other bonus learning aids can be found at his website.

Your Friend in Wealth

Ted Ciuba

Think Your Way To Riches™ Family Style
The Secret Universal Laws of Success

We all know that Life is a rat race. But did you know that it is a rat race that any man, women or child can get out of with the right prosperity thinking and Tools?

Through the pages of this book, Think Your Way To Riches Family Style, I am going to reveal to you the "Twelve Secret Universal Laws" of success that will not only teach you how to get yourself out of the rat race where you are now living, but it also teach your child how to AVOID the rat race all together! Learning these Twelve Secret Universal Laws of Success will get you and your entire family out of the rat race and onto a pathway filled with the abundance of which you are so worthy.

Most people fail to realize that the rat race starts the moment we take our first breath on this earth. Even being a baby is a competitive affair. It is about who crawls, walks, and speaks first in our parent's eyes.

Being at school is competitive. It is about which child is the best behaved, is the best at sports, and who earns the best grades.

Next is college. We pile degree upon degree on ourselves and want our children to do the same, without thinking what message we are "Secretly" conveying to them in the process. Could our society's thought process in fact be promising us a life of abundance and success purely based on conventional education?

If it is, then societies thought process is unintentionally fibbing to every man, woman, and child on the planet. A college education does not guarantee abundance and it definitively is not an instant recipe for success and happiness. If that were the case then all college graduates would be wealthy and all non-graduates would be unsuccessful.

In reality it does not work that way. There are many very prosperous people in the world with no formal college education at all, just as there are also many prosperous people with good college educations. For this reason I am quite happy to point out that a college education has in all probability nothing to do with abundance, prosperity and success whatsoever!

It has to do more with the power within ones own self, to create their own abundance and destiny. The powers that Napoleon Hill and Ted Ciuba share and talk about in Ted's new book "The New Think and Grow Rich," is the power that every man, woman and child has inside themselves to utilize the Twelve Universal Laws of Success and learn that one can create their own wealth even if they do not have a formal education.

Yes, I feel that it takes much more than just a formal education to achieve success, that ANY ONE who utilizes the Twelve Universal Laws of Success and acquires the THINK YOUR WAY TO RICHES mindset can and will be abundant, successful and happy in ALL areas of their lives.

Now before you get upset…it is statistically correct to say that college graduates are higher earners than non-graduates, that much is very true, but does being a higher earner equate to prosperity and abundance in ones life? I feel that answer is a resounding "NO"!

If your objective for piling on the degrees for yourself or your child is to get yourself or your child to amass wealth, then your well intended approach is probably off the mark! It is just ONE of the ingredients that make up the recipe to "Success."

Don't you agree that we owe it to ourselves and our children to have all the ingredients of success? Not just the ones that come from a formal education? Don't you agree that it should be our jobs as parents to help ourselves and our children find the right tools to be the successful adults we all desire to become? College may be one of the right tools for us or our child, but maybe giving ourselves or our child the knowledge to own and operate an internet business may be the tools needed instead?

I truly believe that every man, woman and child is born with different talents and passions which they can utilize to help them become abundant in all areas of their lives, to have the wealth they desire to have to be the person they wish to be, and to have the loving relationships they wish to have.

Yes, locked inside each one of us is the knowledge and power to create our own destinies. The Universal Laws of Success are YOUR "Secret" keys not only to unlock the doors of Prosperity inside yourself, but they will teach you how to keep those doors "Wide Open" and prevent them from ever closing in your own children's lives as well!

Schools and colleges offer academic training, but it's really up to us, the parents, when it comes to abundance training. We are the ones who should learn how to create not only our own dreams, but show our children how to make their dreams become a reality as well.

Children DO NOT have to be adults before they can earn money, start their own business, or start living their dreams. They can be making millions of dollars at an early age when given the tools and knowledge to do so by the adults in their lives.

You do not have to be saddled with the outdated thinking and mindset of our own parents and society. Within you lies the ability to create your own abundant, successful and happy lives and to follow every one of your dreams to completion!

As always "It is choice not chance that makes YOUR destiny!" To live a life of abundance, success and happiness and to follow your dreams or not is totally up to you… learning and under-standing the twelve "Secret Universal Laws of Success" and then teaching them to your children is up to you. Choose wisely and prosper…the choice is now in your hands.

Chapter One

The Law Of Thought And Manifestation

"We are what we think. All that we are arises with our thoughts.
With our thoughts, we make the world."
— *Buddha*

Chapter 1

The world appears to be a certain way. Look out your window; what do you see? Maybe you will see houses, cars, lampposts, trees, sidewalks, and the street. The scene looks solid, with a sense of permanence that makes it feel as though it's always been that way. But think about it for a moment—has it always been that way? Well, of course not. Fifty years ago, it may have been a cornfield. It took effort to transform the landscape into what you see now. The homes had to be built, the streets had to be paved, and even the trees had to be planted. But well before any of this could have happened, someone had to "think it up." Even before a blueprint is drawn for a construction project, the idea begins as a single thought. The reality you perceive outside your living room window, then, had to start as something as ethereal and powerful as a thought.

Throughout the ages, people have wrestled with these questions: What are thoughts? How do we think? Scientists have studied the brain to try to find answers. Thought has been described as a mental process, a chemical process, as brain waves, and now in terms of quantum mechanics. Philosophers have come up with their own concepts, often tying our thoughts to the very core of our being. Sages and mystics advise us to choose our thoughts carefully and to think before we speak, act, or leap. So much has been discussed and written about thought, and yet, for many it remains an elusive concept.

How do you perceive thought? Do you find it difficult to define? If so, don't worry—you certainly are not alone. The day will come when the science of thought is crystal clear. For now, you needn't be concerned with how thought works. All you really need is to see that thought does work to shape our lives. The goal of this chapter is to help you tap into the immense creative power of your thoughts, regardless of your personal definition of thought, regardless of which model you adhere to.

It stands to reason that if thoughts can create tangible things, like neighborhoods, space vehicles, works of fiction, and the intricate innards of a computer, then they certainly can and do work on a much more personal, immediate level as well. We can use our thoughts to create our very lives—our experiences, our choices, our outlook, our direction. And I believe we have a responsibility to teach our children to do just that. Here's the key: Before it can happen "out there," it begins inside of YOU. And so, this is the first Law:

The Universal Law Of Thought And Manifestation: You become what you spend most of your time thinking about. These thoughts create energy, and putting this energy into motion creates your reality.

Think about something long enough and it manifests, or comes to be, as your personal reality. Before you can see it in your life, in the world, you must think it. The mind is a powerful thing. It does not know the difference between what is real and what it perceives to be real. For instance if a person thinks he is Napoleon after awhile he becomes Napoleon. The rest or the world may not see him as Napoleon, but never the less he IS Napoleon in his own mind thus making being Napoleon real for him. So, as you can see, your mind contains a great power to create reality. By thinking of it, you bring it into both your conscious and subconscious minds. This, in turn, creates a certain energy that can take on any number of forms, including desire, intent, excitement, inspiration, hope, commitment, or curiosity. When this energy becomes your focus, it grows and becomes a driving force that ultimately enables you to realize that which you've been thinking.

In other words, your thoughts create your reality. Sometimes you're aware of it, and other times you aren't. By becoming more

4

conscious of the direct connection between your thoughts and your reality, you begin to have greater control of the outcome. This very fact makes it important to teach your child at a young age how to manage their thoughts wisely. Children need to be taught how to NOT be open to the negative thoughts of others. That will give them the power to not create others negative thoughts to be their reality. Parents need to teach their children how to monitor their thoughts so that they may create their own reality of who they are and what they wish to do in life.

What Does This Mean For You?

If you are like the other six and a half billion or so inhabitants of planet Earth, there's some aspect of your life that you'd like to change. Perhaps you'd like to improve your health. Or you'd like to modify your personality to become nicer, more outgoing, or more tolerant of others. Maybe you want to do work that is more meaningful to you, or you'd like to earn a better income. Perhaps you'd like to find someone to share your life with, or you'd like to enjoy more quality time with your loved ones. In order to create a change in your life, you first need to become aware that a mechanism exists to manifest reality from your thoughts.

You may be surprised to learn that, like every other human being, you and your child are already using this mechanism! Question is, are you getting what you think you want and teaching your child to do the same? And the next question is, why not? The answer is that you get what you focus on. If you are focused on what you don't want, that's what you'll get.

Here's an example to illustrate this point. Mary was finishing up college, taking her last courses before getting her bachelor's degree in business administration. Her grades were good, and she was both bright and capable. But she was scared. With this phase of her life coming to an end, she was frightened of what lay "beyond." There was the fear of the unknown, but even greater was her fear that she would end up in a job she disliked.

Mary's life was busy to the point of hectic. In addition to finishing up her studies, she was busy with job applications and interviews. On the outside she appeared poised and confident, but inside she was unknowingly sabotaging herself. Instead of focusing on her dream jobs and visualizing herself working for companies she liked, she worried incessantly. Mary filled her mind with thoughts like these:

"What if nobody makes me an offer?"
"I'll probably get stuck with a stupid job, working with awful people."
"The competition's so fierce. Who will ever hire me?"

These and similar thoughts carried a great deal of weight, unbeknownst to Mary. Instead of thinking thoughts that would generate excitement and synergy to lead her to her ideal job, she developed thoughts that created fear, concern, and a world of negativity. Even though she did well in college and did reasonably well during her interviews, she didn't get offers from the companies she wanted to work for. Her fear-based thoughts created negative energy that held her back. Instead of getting what she thought she wanted, Mary got what consumed her thoughts: very few offers, and only from companies she wasn't thrilled about working for. In the end, her thoughts did create her reality.

If Mary had known what she was doing, she could have taken steps to change the focus of her thoughts. But because she was not aware that our focus becomes our reality, she "accidentally" ended up with the reality she least wanted. Can you relate to Mary's story? Has what happened to her ever happened to you? Most of us have experienced what Mary went through, at some level. And, sad but true, taught our own children by our own actions.

Here is your chance to relearn how to get what you want, and as you yourself learn a new way of thinking, you will be able to teach to your own child this mind set in the process! It begins with clarity of thought. Be completely clear with yourself about what you want. Focus on that, and be sure to do so with a can-do attitude, a sense of confidence, and especially a feeling of love. In this way you begin to create an energy that builds up and thrusts you in that direction. If you focus on what you want but approach it with fear and doubt, you generate self-defeating thoughts that generate a "can't do" type of energy. Instead of moving you in the direction you wish to go, this energy creates a block that holds you back.

Specificity is equally important. The more specific you are about what you want, as well as the more clear you are, the more accurate the resulting manifestation will be. Say, for example, that you desire to eat a cookie. You walk over to your pantry and look inside, and you find a package of generic, store-bought cookies. Not quite what you had in mind, but you pop one into your mouth anyway to get the desire out of your system, and you go about your day.

Now let's get more specific. You want a cookie that's home-made, with natural ingredients. You want to taste its warmth and freshness minutes after it's out of the oven. You want it to have both chocolate chips and dried cranberries. You want it to be on the healthy side, with whole wheat flour and oats. You want the sweet aroma of cookies baking to permeate your entire house, and you know that a little bit of cinnamon will accentuate this wonderful aroma.

At this point, you're not satisfied with the generic cookie in your pantry! You want something very different. You want chocolate chip, cranberry, cinnamon-oatmeal cookies, and you're ready to turn that very specific idea into your reality by getting up and preparing this recipe. It takes more time, but it's exactly what you want, what you visualized, and it brings you greater satisfaction. This cookie example applies to just about anything in you and your child's life. The more you think an idea through, the more certain you are of what you really want, and the more details you attach to that which you desire, the likelier it is that the outcome will be a satisfying one for you. Let's look at another example.

Example: A Weekend Retreat

Earl, Steven, and Jeff looked forward to their upcoming weekend retreat. All three hoped it would be a time of rest, renewal, and personal growth. Each brought with him an open mind, a sense of excitement, and a different idea of what he wanted to take home at the end of the weekend.

Earl wanted to learn better communication skills. He wanted to have a closer relationship with his children and wanted to connect better with his wife. He so desired to be able to talk with her from his heart. He also wanted to be able to talk to his boss without worrying that he might say the wrong thing. This was his focus before and during the retreat.

Steven wanted to learn how to have more fun. He'd been known as "the serious one" and "the responsible one" his whole life. He didn't mind being responsible, but he wanted to give himself permission to do something just for the fun of it once in a while. Everything in his life revolved around being practical. If he read a book, it was never a novel—always a practical "how to." He had a hard time justifying going to the movies with friends, because he felt he should stay home to tune up his car engine or fix the newest leak in his apartment. His responsible nature had helped him advance in his career quickly, and he liked this aspect of himself, but he longed for the freedom to sometimes do things that served no practical purpose whatsoever. This is what he focused on at the retreat.

Jeff wanted to be able to express himself creatively. He had always been highly analytical, and it had served him well. But he felt incomplete, somehow. His mother played the piano beautifully, his father was a wonderful artist, and his sister wrote haunting poetry. In his eyes they were artists, and he

8

felt that somewhere inside himself he was an artist, too. He wanted to discover and express this side of himself. That was his focus over the weekend.

Even though the retreat offered the same program, the same schedule, the same speakers, and the same activities for every attendee, each person got something different out of being there. For some, it was a life-altering weekend. They learned new things about themselves that they'd never known before. Many grew in confidence, courage, patience, forgiveness, and other important areas. A few felt they didn't get much out of the weekend but, even for these individuals, seeds were planted; at some point in the future, when they are ready, they'll continue the work they started at this retreat.

For those who felt they'd grown by leaps and bounds over the weekend, the key was this:

They focused on the growth they desired.

In other words, it wasn't as much what was presented at the retreat, or who spoke, or what activities were offered. Certainly these ingredients were important, but what made the difference in each person's growth level was what the participant came with to the retreat.

Earl brought with him a desire to be a better communicator and the willingness to be open to whatever it would take to learn new communication skills. When he returned to the "real world" after the retreat was over, he remained focused on his goals, and he took action. As a result, he became more honest and assertive with his boss, more conversational and loving with his wife, and more involved in his kids' lives. He learned to improve as a talker and as a listener. His focus created energy, which he put into motion, and which helped him grow in the area of communication, just like he wanted.

Steven discovered the joy of having fun. At the retreat, he learned to relax and to be entertained. A natural leader, he decided to let it go and let others take a leadership position that weekend. Instead, he dove into goofy team-building exercises and spent quiet time reading a novel he'd brought that a friend had recommended to him. He relished singing songs by the campfire, and he even tried something he'd never done before—archery.

None of it served a practical purpose, either at the retreat or back home. That was the whole point. Steven wanted to learn to do something on impulse, just for the fun of it. This was his focus, and like Earl, he succeeded at his goal. His friends and co-workers were happy to see him "let his hair down." He became more creative, more relaxed, and simply more fun to be around.

When he packed for the retreat, Jeff included an artist's sketchbook and a high-quality set of colored pencils. He'd had these for quite some time, but the pages of his sketchbook were empty and the pencils were still sharp, since he'd never found (or made) the time to try his hand at art. Partly it was because of fear, since success was very important to him and he didn't want to try art if he was simply going to fail. And partly it was reluctance. Art was always in the back of his mind, but he consistently chose to remain on the technical path rather than explore his creative side. Perhaps that just felt safer to him.

At the retreat, he finally gave himself permission to draw and color. People looking over his shoulder were immensely impressed by his artwork and couldn't believe that he'd never taken an art class before. This boosted his confidence. He spent most of the weekend sketching in his book. By the time he went home, he was hooked. He had found a wonderful way to relax and unwind. He discovered that drawing even helped him whenever he got stuck on a challenging problem at work. It was the perfect outlet, and at the same time it seemed to stimulate the part of his brain that sought solutions to technical problems.

Each person left the retreat with something completely different. Each one created his specific reality based on what he chose to focus on. Each one grew, because each person had the courage to give energy to thought, and to put that energy into motion. By thinking about what they wanted most, and giving themselves permission to bring that which they desired into their lives, they used the Law of Thought and Manifestation to change and grow, in just one weekend.

The Law At Work In Your Life

In many ways, life is like a weekend retreat, but we don't fully realize it. At any given moment, we have the opportunity to evaluate who we are, where we are, where we are headed, and who we really want to be. But until we give ourselves permission to perform this self-evaluation, we continue with "business as usual."

What happens then? We feel like were stuck in a rut. We become Depressed and Unhappy with our situation. We may feel Unmotivated and Enslaved.

Look at the Law again:

You become what you spend most of your time thinking about. These thoughts create energy, and putting this energy into motion creates your reality.

If you feel you are stuck, depressed, unhappy, unmotivated, even enslaved, then you are thinking these thoughts, and you are creating energy that keeps you in the particular state you're thinking about. In other words, you are sabotaging yourself, perhaps without even realizing it. Also, start to notice the people you are around. If you are around people who are sad, depressed, unhappy, you will tend to feel the same way. Have you ever noticed that people who accept these feelings tend to bring everyone down around them? Don't accept these feeling in yourself or instill them in your child. I myself have learned not to let others tell me their negative thoughts.

When I did learn not to accept negative emotions from others it was a life altering experience for me. It freed me of ever wanting to share what I call my own emotional vomit with anyone. This awareness of how emotionally draining other people's energy can be happened to come to me during a conversation with a good friend of mine. I have a friend whose husband was always treating her badly. She would call to tell me all the details of how awful her life was. I started to notice that when my friend called I would think about her problems all day long then when my own husband came home I tended to be moody with him. I realized that by thinking about my friends' negative relationship I was starting to manifest problems in my own relationship. Why? Because I was unconsciously putting one of the other Universal Laws, the Law of Attraction into motion. The Law of Attraction states that what you think about, and feel, you attract to you, well, having a bad relationship with my own husband was not what I wanted to attract at all! So the next time my friend called I said, Nancy before start our chat, I have something to ask you. Is there anything I can do for you to help you? Lend you money or give you a place to stay? She said no. I proceeded to asked her if she felt what she was about to tell me would make me feel bad?

She said yes, her husband had hit her again. I then said something that surprised even me. I said do you like me? She said of course, how could you dare ask me such question? Because if you liked me you would NOT tell me things that make me feel bad, especially if I can not help you. Sharing your emotional baggage with me, does not allow me or you to feel the emotional happiness of which we are both worthy.

From that day forward I made a pact with myself that I would not except or share emotional baggage with anyone, and from that day forward my friend stopped calling to tell me her problems. Nancy started taking the reasonability of manifesting a new relationship in her life. Yes, that one eye opening conversation changed both our lives for the better.

The antidote here is quite simple: change what you are thinking.

Do you want to feel free, engaged in life, pumped up, happy with your situation, motivated, unencumbered? Then think this way! When you create these thoughts, and spend a great deal of time with them, they will manifest. You will create energy associated with these particular thoughts. Start to surround yourself with people who also think this way, so that you will not be dragged down by their negative emotions. And that energy will create your reality accordingly.

To make the Law of Thought and Manifestation work for you and your child, try these steps: The visualization CD will help you and your child with this exercise:

1 *Clear your mind of all thoughts. You may wish to close your eyes to accomplish this.*

2 *Practice deep breathing. Breathe in, breathe out. Do this for a good five to ten minutes, and notice how relaxed you become.*

3 *Next, picture yourself being who you want to become, or doing something you find rewarding. Feel the positive feelings and thoughts generated by picturing this image.*

4 *Allow your thoughts to move into other areas, but keep them positive, upbeat, and affirming. Explore as many areas as you wish, maintaining a positive, proactive, can-do attitude.*

5 *When negative thoughts (related to can't, shouldn't, worries, fears, and so on) try to enter the scene, gently*

push them away. Actually visualize yourself softly pushing them away from you, and then watch them drift away. Keep yourself detached and unconcerned as these thoughts move towards the horizon. Soon you no longer see them clearly. Soon they simply vanish.

6 *Now, return to the pleasant thoughts you were having prior to this interruption. Focus on them. Feel how your body reacts pleasantly to these thoughts and images. You may feel a sense of love, joy, happiness, excitement, anticipation, enthusiasm, or empowerment. Hold on to these feelings and internalize them for as long as you can.*

Once you have practiced these six steps it will become easier and easier for you to invite helpful thoughts into your life and "push away" thoughts that have no place in your life. Playing the visualization CD often will help both you and your child to apply this six-step technique more easily and quickly to your subconscious minds. With practice and focus, you and your child will soon learn how to make the Law of Thought and Manifestation work for you, even if you've been living your whole life from a place of fear and doubt. You will soon be able to create empowering, loving thoughts at will. These forces will create a beneficial sort of energy, and this energy will in turn make it easier for you and your child to focus on the right things.

Give it a try—what have you got to lose?

Affirmations To Use

An affirmation is a statement that you say to yourself in order to help you along your journey. Children should be taught how to say affirmations at a young age. Even ones as simple as, "I am happy,' will be a powerful affirmation for a child. Affirmations can help you reach goals, modify the pattern of your thinking, offer you support as you strive towards a dream, and give you positive feedback to uplift you every step of the way. Use them freely and often. Say them to yourself every day, many times a day. Post them throughout your home or office. Children often have fun writing their affirmations on bright colored sticky note pads. Write them down and read them back to yourself, and with your child every night, every morning, or whenever it's most convenient for you. Don't forget to ask your child where they would like to place their affirmations. Many children like to place them on the bathroom mirror or the refrigerator. One child I know likes to put his affirmations under his pillow. That way it's the first thing he recites when he wakes up, and the last thing he recites before he falls asleep.

The following affirmations can help you internalize the Universal Law of Thought and Manifestation:

> **Affirmation 1:** My thoughts matter. I own my thoughts. I own responsibility for what I think.
>
> **Affirmation 2:** With my thoughts, I can improve my life, my home, my world.
>
> **Affirmation 3:** I choose to focus on thoughts that empower, embrace, uphold, uplift, and enlighten.
>
> **Affirmation 4:** With my thoughts, I can create a roadmap to follow which will take me to my goals.
>
> **Childs Affirmation:** If it is good for me, I will think it.

Now you and your child should try your hand at creating affirmations. Let your child be creative when making up their affirmation. Even if it's something crazy like, 'I can talk to animals.' Now get started writing down your affirmations then remember to practice reciting them on a daily basis, to start utilizing the Law of Thought and Manifestation. Feel free to start an affirmations journal. Or jot down your child's and your affirmations on note cards and keep them handy to say anytime.

Your goal is to repeat your personal affirmations, and the ones printed here and in the next chapters, often and regularly. When you say them, mean them. Believe them completely. In this way, you reprogram your thinking and your psyche, enabling you to embrace the Twelve Laws presented to you in this book.

Exercises To Try With Your Child

In addition to saying words out loud that will align you with the Law of Thought and Manifestation, you can do other exercises to get all of you—your body, your mind, your emotions, your spirit, your energy, your motivation, your imagination—more in tune with this Universal Law. Try the following. You may want to repeat one, two, or all three exercises again and again. Doing these with your children is a perfect way to bond with them and get to know them even better. Just do the ones with your child that you feel comfortable with and according to your child's age. Make a game out of them when you are doing them with your child so that they enjoy this learning process with you. Who knows, your child just might surprise you and have a thing or two to teach you in the process. If one doesn't yield the results you want the first time around, don't worry. Leave it alone for a while. Come back to it later, when you're ready to try again.

1 **Analyze An Accomplishment.** Then ask your child to do the same. Is there someone you admire greatly? Someone you studied while in school or a person you consider a hero? What did this person accomplish? How much do you know about this person? For a young child to make this exercise simple just ask them who their hero is and why they are their hero? Many young children say mom, dad, or grandparent on this one. If they do, you

are sure to learn a lot about how your child perceives you through this exercise.

Take a trip to your local library. Or surf the Internet, doing a search on this person. Read the books or articles you find about your hero. Once you're well versed in his or her story—the challenges that were overcome, the achievements reached, the highs and the lows this person experienced—take a closer look. Where did the person get the idea to do what she or he did? How did the inspiration or motivation come about?

Your job here is to trace the accomplishment back to the original idea. Then, figure out what your hero did to take that first thought and develop it, ultimately bringing it out into the physical realm. How did your hero go from thinking it up to actually creating it in his or her life? Let your child's imagination go wild here. It is sure to bring a smile to your face.

2 **Take A Walk Of Discovery.** Go for a walk with your child, either in your neighborhood or perhaps near a playground or park. Look around at everything you see as you walk—the park bench, the streetlight, the buildings, the statues or other works of art. For everything that you see, ask your child these questions, who made this? Who created, designed, and developed this?

Let your child's imagination go with it. Ask them to Picture how the park bench, for example, came to be. Who thought of it? Why? How did that person design it? Why this particular look? Why this location? Doing this with your child teaches them how to think for themselves. Never tell them they have a wrong answer. Let them think out of the box, and ask them why they answered in the way they did.

Perform this exercise for other items you see. In your imagination, trace each object from thought to manifestation.

3 **Practice Thinking & Manifesting.** Now it's time for you and your child to put the Law into practice. Look around your home. Take a close, careful look. While you look around, give thanks for that which you have, material and non-material blessings alike (we'll cover gratitude in great detail in another chapter, but it's good to start practicing now having a grateful heart).

After you've expressed your gratitude, think of a change. It could be a new arrangement of your furniture. It could be rearranging the pictures on the wall. It could be setting out a pretty bowl with an assortment of fruit as a centerpiece for your kitchen table. Or perhaps creating a different centerpiece—a lovely vase with fresh flowers from your yard. If you are nervous about doing this exercise with a young child, why not allow them to make the changes in their own room instead of the whole house?

Now that you've thought it, take the next step—make it so. Do what you need to do to manifest your thoughts. Rearrange the furniture or the pictures on your wall. Set out that bowl of fruit or the flower arrangement.

Stand back and look at what you've just created. How does it change your mood? How do you like your new reality you just created? Does it need a little tweaking? If so, go for it. Fix it up just the way you like it. Let your child be creative as you do this exercise together, even if they want to do something as simple as put dandelions in the flower vase. Let them. Who knows… they might be an interior designer some day!

Now that you've practiced manifesting your external reality, rest assured that in the same way, you can manifest your internal reality. With your thoughts you can start to change whatever you wish, be it on the outside, or on the inside. The choice and the power are yours, so why not do as I do. Get up each day and recite out loud this statement: 'All is well in my world. Why? Because it's my world and I choose to make it the world I want it to be.'

Summing It Up

Even though everything appears solid, it had to be thought of first before it was made.

We can use our thoughts to create our lives, including our experiences, our choices, our outlook, and our direction.

When you think about something long enough it becomes your personal reality.

To create a change in your life, you need to know that there's a mechanism to manifest reality from your thoughts.

You get what you focus on.

It's choice not chance that makes your destiny.

Be completely clear about what you want.

The more specific you are about what you want, as well as the clearer you are, the more accurate the resulting manifestation will be.

When you and your child start to create empowering, loving thoughts, a beneficial sort of energy results and this energy in turn makes it easier for you to focus on the right things.

Chapter Two

The Law Of Desire For Change

*"In my experience, there is only one motivation, and that is desire.
No reasons or principle contain it or stand against it."*
— Jane Smiley

Chapter 2

Did you ever want something with all your might when you were a child? You fervently wished for it, you thought about it day and night, perhaps you even asked Santa for it. The object of your desire may have been a doll, a truck, a telescope, a particular book. Perhaps you obsessed over it the way young Ralphie dreams of owning a Red Ryder BB gun in the classic movie, A Christmas Story. Even though everyone tells him, "You'll shoot your eye out," Ralphie does, indeed, get his coveted Red Ryder in the end.

Did you get the object of your desire when you were a child? If not, did you get it at a later point in your life?

I know a lady in her forties (we'll call her "Anna") who desperately wanted a Barbie doll when she was a little girl. Her parents worked hard and provided their children with essentials—food, clothes, shelter, school supplies—but there was little money left over for toys. As a result, her parents bought toys that were inexpensive and more educational in nature, since they prized education, seeing it as an avenue for a better life for their children's future.

Sometimes a trip down a discount store's toy aisle meant a new puzzle or brain-stimulating board game to bring home, perhaps chess or Scrabble. But every time, Anna's eyes would gravitate towards the fashionable dolls with their perfect smiles and bright shiny clothes. She desired a Barbie with all her might, but she never asked for one. She had too much pride to ask. She also respected her parents, loved them dearly, and knew they simply didn't have the funds for such frivolities.

The years passed and Anna grew from a girl to a teenager to an adult, forgetting all about the doll she so wanted as a child.

She went to college, launched her engineering career, and married. After a few years she became pregnant; the ultrasound revealed that her firstborn was a daughter. At the baby shower, Anna and her husband opened all sorts of wonderful gifts—baby blankets, adorable pink outfits, practical tools of the trade, cute teddy bears.

But there was also a gift that seemed unusual, even out of place at a baby shower: a fashion Barbie doll. While most of the shower guests looked at the doll quizzically, Anna smiled gratefully. Even though it was meant for her little girl, she knew it'd be a few years before her daughter would be old enough to play with it. Meanwhile, Anna would enjoy the doll as her own Barbie, the one she wished for as a child. Her desire materialized into reality when she least expected it.

When I myself was a young child I loved all animals but my mother was not fond of pets.

I desired to have pets with all of my heart. My grandmother asked me once if my mom and dad would let me have just one pet what would it be. Well, I thought about if for a while and decided that if I could have only one pet it would have to be a big one. I wanted to have a big cat like a lion. If I had a lion I could ride on it like a horse, or swim with in the lake, and even sit way up in a tree with it. I thought about that big cat for years and even pretended that I had an invisible one to play with. Yes, I desired to have that big lion to play with and thought about it constantly for almost three years. Then as I grew older, went off to school, I forgot all about my desire to have a big cat to play with. Years went by, I got married, raised children of my own. Then out of the blue I did end up with a large cat to play with. It was a mountain lion called Hercules. I may not have manifested the pet I desired to be my reality as a child, but I manifested him just the same. It's just that my manifesting thoughts of a big lion came to me in physical form when I was older. So never give up on the things you desire to have or do in your life. They will manifest when you least expect it some-times, just like my lion Hercules.

This brings us to our second Universal Law:

The Universal Law Of Desire For Change: To change your life, you must change your thinking. Your heart-felt desire is to be the focus of your thinking.

Children usually do not have the means or resources to change their lives. They rely greatly on support from their guardians or teachers. If there is a child in your life who desires to bring about change, one that might not be your own child, please consider helping him or her out by sharing this book with their parents, or even much in the way the school teacher Barbara Vogel helped her fifth grade students accomplish something even adults considered "impossible."

While reading the newspaper at home, Barbara came across an article that revealed the modern-day practice of slavery in the Sudan. Shocked and deeply saddened, she made a personal commitment then and there to do something about it. She also decided that she needed to share this article with her students, who'd just finished an American history unit on slavery.

Barbara read the article aloud in class, and her students learned of the abuse and denigration experienced by those enslaved in the Sudan—including young children. They couldn't believe what they were hearing. By the time Barbara was done reading the piece, many of them had tears streaming down their faces. After a moment or two of stunned silence, one child spoke up: "What are we going to do about this?" The entire class decided they could not "do nothing" while the people of Sudan suffered. Their consciences would not let them ignore the problem.

The class proceeded to write letters to politicians and celebrities. They sold lemonade and donated their allowance money, thus raising funds to help free slaves through a charitable organization working in the region. With Barbara's full support, the children did everything in their power to raise awareness of something they deeply felt was wrong. They became young abolitionists.

Their efforts led them to Washington D.C., where some of them spoke with then Secretary of State Madeleine Albright, and some even testified before members of Congress. These children succeeded not only in freeing real people caught in the grip of slavery, but also in bringing their plight to the attention of political leaders who finally listened. And all this began from a very basic desire—a desire that emanated from these fifth grade student's tears and broken hearts, a desire that other children around the world could live in dignity and freedom. It began with a desire for change.

What Does This Mean For You and your child?

If children, with limited resources and little power, can accomplish as much as these young students did, you can be sure that you are capable of just as much, and more. It begins with a sincere, deep desire for change. Think of what you would like to change: Then ask your child what they may like to change in their lives and why they may want to change it. Being able to keep an open communication with our children is important. You could even ask them these questions on a car ride to keep their minds active. What about…

- *Your present life circumstances?*

- *Your outlook on life?*

- *A personal trait or characteristic?*

- *Your career?*

- *Your attitude?*

- *Your community?*

- *Your world?*

These are not unrealistic goals. You can enact change in any capacity you wish. It begins with listening to your heart's desire. You as a parent should look inside yourself beyond any walls you may have constructed for self-protection; what do you see? What ambitions, wishes, and desires do you find living within you?

It is very possible that you have "forgotten" your desires, but trust that this is only temporary. They remain within you, even if they are buried deeply. You can bring them to the surface by spending time each day reflecting upon what you might desire, asking yourself questions such as:

- *What did I used to dream about?*

- *When did I forget my heart's dreams?*

- *How might I nurture myself to bring them back?*

- *How have my dreams changed?*

- *If there were no limits, what do I truly desire now?*

- *What do I fervently wish for?*

You may find it helpful to keep a notepad next to your bed or at your desk. Then, as you ponder these questions and answers start to appear, write them down. By doing this you will unlock the hidden dreams and desires that have been residing dormant inside yourself. At the end of two weeks, read back your entries. A picture will begin to form, reminding you of your deepest wishes. This is the first step: Know with clarity what it is that you desire. When you as a parent know these truths within yourself, you will be able to give your child the wisdom to always keep their dreams and true desires alive. Before we move on to the next step, let's look at another example that illustrates how the Law of Desire for Change works.

Example: "I Need A Change!"

Sandra had been married for 17 years. She deeply loved her husband and their three children and devoted herself to taking care of them, but she felt a strong sense of discontentment with her present life. There was nothing she could pinpoint; her kids were growing up nicely and doing fine in school and in their personal lives. Her husband was doing well in his career. The two of them were close and enjoyed time together. She knew that many people would envy what she had. So why was she so discontented with herself?

When her feelings began to skirt dangerously close to depression, Sandra realized she had to do something. She confided in a close friend, who recommended she see a particular therapist. Hesitantly, Sandra picked up the phone and scheduled an appointment.

Slowly but steadily, she and her therapist began to get to the root of her discontent. At first, Sandra just kept saying, "I'm not happy with myself, with my life. I need a change. I need a change!" But when pressed for more, she was stuck—she didn't know what to change. She didn't know what would make her happier. After a few weeks of working with her therapist, she began to get a better picture of what was going on. Sandra wasn't happy because, beyond being wife and mother (roles which were very important to her and of which she was extremely proud) she had nothing for herself. When her kids left home, what would she have left? What would she occupy her time with? Tending to her husband, as wonderful as he was, and to the house and yard just wasn't enough. She needed something else.

Sandra was actually relieved to learn that this was the problem; she had worried before about what "change" might mean—leaving her husband? Going back to college to finish her degree?

Joining a convent? She didn't want to do anything like that. To learn that she didn't have to was a relief. All she needed was something for herself. She did not need to disrupt her family or throw away what she already had, which was precious to her.

The next step was a little harder; she needed to discover what would give her daily life more meaning. What would make her more complete? Again, progress was slow at first. But in time, exciting possibilities opened up, because she allowed herself to think of them, to dream. Finally, Sandra had a clear picture in her mind of the changes she wanted for herself:

1 *To work outside of the home, preferably with children, because she liked kids and she felt she had a gift—an ability to relate to them on their level.*

2 *To bring in some income.*

3 *To work part-time so that she could be home when her children were home.*

With these goals in mind, she set off to find work that would meet her desires and requirements. She was amazed that her search panned out quickly—within a month, she was working at an elementary school as a classroom assistant. The position met her criteria beautifully. Sandra was happy to finally have something for herself. Now at the dinner table, when she listened to her children's stories about school and her husband's tales of work, she could add to the mix by sharing funny stories from her job. She felt whole.

And it all came about because she finally gave herself permission to truly focus on her desire for change. She did it fully in the context of love, without fear.

The Law At Work In Your Life

It begins with the seeds of desire that's in you and your child's heart. You want to change something in your life. Maybe you know exactly what. Maybe you have no clue, at least not yet. It's possible that you know you want to change something simply because you're feeling dissatisfied, or detached, or you've stopped feeling altogether. Do not despair. Instead, congratulate yourself for picking up on these clues. Something's gotta change, right?

The beauty of Universal Laws is that they work, wherever you may be on your life journey. All you need to do is remain open to the possibilities. Have an open mind and an open heart. Have faith, and trust that there is a process that backs up each and every one of these Universal Laws, including the Law of Desire for Change. Take a second look at this Law:

To change your life, you must change your thinking. Your heartfelt desire is to be the focus of your thinking.

When's the last time you as a parent took the time to focus on what you truly, genuinely desire? It is true that with all of the busy-ness of life and our many obligations and responsibilities, it is sometimes difficult to find, or make, the time to focus on our heart's desire. But as a parent if you can't seem to find the time to do this for yourself, how on earth will you find the time to teach this valuable lesson to your child? Children learn from the example set by parents, Take a minute and think about what your daily actions are teaching your child. Do they say, I am too busy to focus on what I desire to do in life, or maybe that, I am just too busy to enjoy my life? Really take a moment and ask yourself if the life you are living is the life you would want your child to live. If you said YES, that's fantastic. If not then you must change your thinking. Changing your thinking will naturally result in a change in your life.

You can put the Law of Desire for Change to work in your life and teach it to your child   by following these six steps:

1 *Pick a quiet moment when you and your child can be alone with your thoughts, without distractions or interruptions. Choose the time of day that works best for you both, such as when you first wake up, or in the moments before going to bed. Other possibilities include when you are taking a bath or shower, when you are cooking, or when you are sharing the responsibility of taking your dog out for a walk.*

2 *Go within. And teach your child how to do the same. Teach them how to talk to themselves inside their own thoughts. Now, rediscover your core, where your spirit resides. Connect with your spirit and initiate a dialogue, asking yourself, Am I who I need to be at this point in time?*

3 *Go into your heart. Again, do a "reality check." Ask yourself, am I taking care of my heart's desire? Ask your child to ask themselves if they are happy and living the life they wish to. If a child is very young ask them the question yourself and await their answers.*

4 *Search your soul thoroughly Ask yourself honestly what you are happy, satisfied, and content with, and what you're less than happy with. Then ask your child these questions. Then, go deeper. Go to the root. What is it that you wish to accomplish that you've not yet addressed? What would you like to learn or become that you haven't given yourself permission to yet? Then when you have the answers to these question yourself, ask your child what they want to learn or become.*

5 Next go into your mind. Check your thinking. Are you supporting your dreams and heart's desire through your thinking? Are you treating yourself with kindness and forgiveness? How about others, are you treating them in the spirit of kindness and forgiveness? If not, why not? Is there something in your thinking that is holding you back in any way? After you have found these answers yourself, ask your child the same questions.

6 Now that you've done a full analysis of your current state of being, ask yourself this important question: If I could change one thing today, what would it be? What is the starting point for the change I desire to be? Once again, after you have done this for you, then ask your child those questions.

This is all you need to do at any given time. You and your child just need to start with ONE thing you would like to change and Work on that. Never mind the rest. It's not time to work on the other stuff yet. Focus on the one thing you've pinpointed that you need to change today in your attitude, in your thinking, in your approach, or in your perception. Then put your energy on making that one change. Once you and your child have enacted that one change, you both will have accomplished perhaps more than you realize.

The next time you and your child perform this self-analysis, you'll come up with another area where change will do you good. By approaching the process one change at a time, and putting all of your focus and energy on that one without even considering others, you will make steady progress. It will be a very do-able venture for both of you. An exciting and fun adventure awaits you!

Affirmations To Use

To help you integrate the Universal Law of Desire for Change into you and your child's life, try repeating the following affirmations to yourself. They will give you both strength and courage to embrace change as an exciting opportunity. They will also give you both the confidence to take those first steps towards discovering what you would like to change, how best to enact change, and how to continue forward on your chosen paths.

Some people need to give themselves permission to make changes in life. I would venture to say that most people need to give themselves that level of permission. Like Sandra in our earlier example, deep down they feel they might let others down if they change the "status quo," or they feel it might be selfish to think about themselves. The truth is that when you are happy and fulfilled doing what you love to do, that is when you are able to best serve those whom you love.

I would like to give you and your child the permission to discover who you are, and what you are meant to do. Now, I ask that you and your child give yourself that permission also. Go ahead, it's OK. Give yourself permission to look into your heart and discover the road you seek to travel. In order to get from point A to point B, you will need to change, to grow, to take one step, then a second, and a third, and so on. Just take one step at a time.

Make your heartfelt desire the focus of your thinking. As you and your child begin to create that shift in your lives, say the following affirmations aloud.

> **Affirmation 1:** There is an avenue for bettering my existence, and it is called change… Change is my tool of choice for a better life.

Affirmation 2: I am comfortable making the right changes in my life… The choice is mine.

Affirmation 3: Change is a beautiful means for getting unstuck and moving forward with my plans, my joy, my purpose, my life.

Affirmation 4: I have the courage to change my thinking in a way that aligns me better with what I want to do in my life.

Childs Affirmation: I can change and be who I want to be.

If you or your child wants to personalize any of these affirmations, by all means feel free to do so. Keep the basic idea and intent the same, but change the words around to fit your needs and your personality, if you wish.

In addition, make up your own. Repeat affirmations frequently. Remember, that you and your child are conditioning your whole selves. You are reprogramming yourselves right down to the cellular level. You are using affirmations to empower yourselves and benefit from the Law of Desire for Change.

Exercises To Try With Your Child

Once again, your re-conditioning will be much more powerful if you and your child take a holistic approach. By engaging and involving your entire selves, your use of this Universal Law will be more effective, and your results will be more enduring. Try the following exercises with your child to help you fully internalize the Law of Desire for Change. As always do these exercises with your Child's age in mind and make it very simple for them.

1 **Create Your Work Of Art** by creating a dream board together. How you create this dream board will be up to

you and your child. There is not a right or wrong way to make your dream boards. You can create a simple pencil drawing and add color with crayons or colored pencils if you like. You can use paint and a paintbrush. You can make a sculpture out of clay. You can do computer art, or you can cut pictures out of magazines and glue them onto poster board or construction paper. Again, the choice is entirely yours. You are making your own dream board so that every time you look at your dream board you will feel your dreams coming true. Put your dream board where you look at it OFTEN throughout the day.

Watch how creative your child can be at this. They are often masters of knowing what they want. A trip to Disney World, a new iPod, a pony or, for an older child, the money to go on spring break with their friends. Feel free to put words on your dream board like, I am great, I am happy, I am beautiful, and anything that makes you feel good about you.

The point of this exercise is for you and your child to create a work of art that reflects your heart's desires. This hands-on approach will help you both to focus on what it is that you desire most. You will first go within to explore your thoughts, feelings, and emotions. Then you will choose your artistic means of expression. And finally, you will create a work of art that best reflects that which you both desire. Why not make a family dream board after you make your own personal dream boards. Place on it the things you want to manifest as a family. Like a vacation, new boat, new house, or even world peace. What a fun way for you and your family to focus on manifesting together. With your whole family putting their energy on this dream board I am sure they will manifest faster.

Now let's take it to the next level. After you finish creating a representation of your heart's desire, then you and your child might want to add something to it that reflects a change in your thinking, perception, or attitude that will create a change for you for the better. If you feel comfortable doing so, share your work with someone you trust. This part is completely optional and up to you. You need not share it with anyone other than yourself.

2 **Rethink It.** To change your life, you have to change your thinking, so why not practice? Choose an issue you may have heard about in the news recently, or that your community is facing. Ponder for a moment your thoughts on this issue. Next, turn it around. What about the people on the other side of the issue? Why do they feel the way they do? What life experiences could they have had to have them reach the conclusion they've come to? This thinking becomes a great way to teach your child how to solve problems. Ask them what they would do and why. Who knows, they may come up with an answer to create world peace.

Practice doing this with other issues. This exercise helps you and your children accomplish a couple of things. First, it makes you expand your minds and think about other answers you may not have considered yet. And just as importantly, it enables you to take the side of someone you don't know, which can help you grow in empathy and compassion—two qualities that will serve you well as you learn to master all of the Universal Laws.

Now take it one step further. Why do you feel the way you do about certain issues? What life experiences have led you to feel this way? What events or circumstances might cause you to change your mind? This part of the exercise will help you and your child to stretch your minds, making you a more flexible, open-minded individual.

3 **Concentration.** Focusing your thoughts on what you truly desire—to be in a different line of work, for exam-

ple, or to be more patient with everyone you encounter—takes a certain measure of discipline. It takes concentration. You can practice focusing and concentrating through this exercise.

Write down five words that describe your ideal life. You should only write down one or two words for a young child. They don't have to be in any particular order; write them down randomly as they come to you. Now, concentrate on these words for a moment to memorize them. Turn your sheet of paper over, and write down the five words you've just memorized.

Next add five more words. Memorize these. On another sheet of paper, write all ten words that you've just memorized.

This is a bit more challenging now. Add ten more words to describe your desired life. Take just a few seconds to memorize these, but really focus. Then cover up all the words you've written, or get another piece of paper, and write down from memory all twenty words that you thought of.

This exercise helps you and your child to practice focusing on what you want and gives you a little bit of practice in concentration. To finish up, write a short story with your child (a couple of paragraphs is fine, but make it longer if you wish) incorporating all the words you came up with. The story is of your choosing. Just make sure it ties into your heart's desire in some way. Feel free to write a story for yourself then one for your child. Older children will be able to write their own stories, Do this exercise at least once a month to help with your concentration. Why not have even more fun with this exercise and make a family story book out of the stories. That way you can share the stories you have written over and over again with your children and later even your grandchildren.

Summing It Up

Great things—exciting projects, charitable ventures, and a new direction in life—begin with a desire for change.

Start by listening to your heart's desire. And teach your child to do the same.

If you have "forgotten" your desires, trust that this is a temporary condition. They remain within you.

You and your child can bring your buried, forgotten desires to the surface by spending time each day reflecting upon what it is that you might wish for.

Soon a picture will begin to form, reminding you of your deepest wishes.

With practice, you and your child will know with clarity what you desire.

First focus on what you truly, genuinely desire. Then, change your thinking.

You and your child should start with one thing you would like to change, and focus your attention and energy on that.

You must both give yourself permission to follow your heart's desire.

Chapter
Three

The Law Of Vision
And Goals

*"Ordinary people believe only in the possible. Extraordinary people
visualize not what is possible or probable, But rather what is impossible.
And by visualizing the impossible, They begin to see it as possible."*
— Cherie Carter-Scott

Chapter 3

If you watch competitive figure skating, skiing, gymnastics, or almost any other sport, you've no doubt seen an interesting phenomenon. Just before the gymnast gets on stage to perform a routine, or the skier leaves the gate to race down the mountain, or the skating couple emerges onto the ice, each athlete goes through a mental exercise. You'll see the athletes close their eyes and focus deeply, going through every step of the routine or every ski turn in their mind. Before going out to compete, each athlete visualizes the performance, or the race, dozens or even hundreds of times. It's a mental practice run, and it's extremely powerful. Teaching your child how to do this will surely give them a winners mind set in life.

People use this effective technique in other lines of work as well. A business executive preparing to give a key company presentation runs through the talk in her mind several times before actually giving it. A skydiver mentally runs through the necessary steps—leaping, quickly getting into the right freefall position, opening the parachute, steering the parachute, preparing for landing, and finally, landing safely—many, many times before jumping out of the airplane. Even a new parent goes over each individual step mentally before giving baby his first bath.

Why? What's so important about going through a multi-step process in your mind before actually doing it? The answer is simple: practice makes perfect, whether it's in the physical realm or in the mental domain. Visualization is a very useful technique that enables you to see results before they happen. It allows you to do two or ten or fifty trial runs, all from the safety, comfort, and convenience of your mind.

Every time you do another mental trial run, something remarkable happens: your mind works to program the cells of your body and imprints an energy pattern of a successful outcome into your psyche. When you see it in your mind, you believe it. Your body records it, your energy field changes, and when the time comes to perform, you respond accordingly. Visualization gives you a distinct advantage.

When we envision ourselves going after our goals and achieving them, we're training ourselves. We're preparing ourselves for future success, in both the immediate future (just a breath ahead of the present) and in the more distant future. That's what the third Law is about.

The Universal Law Of Vision and Goals: What you see clearly in your thoughts is what you get in your life experiences. Visualize yourself achieving a goal, and you form a bridge to reaching that goal.

Setting goals gives you something to strive for. Seeing yourself going after these goals—and reaching them—sets up a framework of success in your mind. The more you visualize yourself achieving, in great detail, the more you prepare and program yourself for making this your reality. This is the mind set each parent should teach their child to have at an early age, if they want them to acquire the mind set of a winner. The mind set they will need to achieve, giving them the ability to create a life they are wishing to live.

What does visualization mean, exactly? It's the process of creating internal mental images. It is both creative and practical. You use your imagination to envision something that hasn't happened yet. Often when you visualize, you do so in a systematic, step-by-step manner. The clearer you can see things in your thoughts, the clearer your results.

Srinivasa Ramanujan was born in 1887 in southern India (where, by the way, the number zero was invented, or perhaps more accurately, discovered; yes, the concept of zero was also developed by the Maya). This young man was one of the most adept mathematicians of his era, brilliant with number theories, infinite series, and countless mathematical functions. Many of the formulas he developed only he fully understood at the time, but his unique brand of math is now finding practical applications in computer science, chemistry, and physics, especially in the study of atomic and molecular structure. No doubt about it, he was well ahead of his time.

And he was consumed by mathematics, sometimes working out highly advanced equations for thirty hours straight before collapsing into exhausted sleep. One thing that set Srinivasa apart from other eminent mathematicians was his amazing ability to visualize incredibly complicated, long formulas and processes in his mind in tremendous detail. He sometimes would say that answers to complex problems were presented to him in his dreams (another form of mental visualization) by the Goddess Namagiri of Namakkal, a Hindu goddess of creativity and knowledge. Unlike those who viewed mathematics as mere mental computations, the intuitive and spiritual Srinivasa was crystal clear about the source of his mathematical prowess. He said, "An equation for me has no meaning, unless it expresses a thought of the God."

Indeed, geniuses possess a gift that allows them access to the divine. Brilliant musicians, artists, scientists, theorists, and other great thinkers and doers are able to tap into something special, to "see beyond," and that seeing takes place in the mind's eye. Answers appear to the person intuitively, often utilizing some form of visualization.

If athletes and business executives, mathematicians and musicians can first see thoughts clearly in their minds, then apply these thoughts to achieve goals and reach new horizons in their chosen paths, then it makes sense that a mechanism exists to make this possible. It has to. So giving our children the keys to learn how to use this mind set will surly be a great gift.

It also stands to reason that if such a mechanism exists, then every one of us should be able to access it. What's more, we as parents can learn to use this mechanism to affect our life experiences in a positive way. Then we can empower our children by giving them the wisdom on how to access it within their own self. The mechanisms of visualization and goal-setting can help each of us transform our lives from ho-hum to holy, from ordinary to completely extraordinary.

What Does This Mean For You?

How many times have you as a parent wished for help finishing a project, or starting one? How often have you desired to "see" the outcome of your actions before taking them? The wonderful thing about the Law of Vision and Goals is that you can get that help you want and also show your child how to do so at any stage of a project, be it beginning, middle, or end, and you can see results before doing anything, just by using and mastering this Universal Law. The better you and your child can get at visualizing your goals, the better this Law will work for you both.

Look at these real-life examples of people who've successfully visualized an outcome before completing the process:

1 J.K. Rowling, author of the immensely successful Harry Potter book series, thought up her character while riding aboard a train. She has said, "Harry just strolled into my head fully formed."

2 A young Canadian man who goes by the name of Adam works as a distant energy healer. He has the uncanny ability to visualize three-dimensional holographic views of the people he works with. He "sees" their illnesses and health conditions holographiacally, and then he's able to go in and do repairs energetically.

3 Madam C. J. Walker was a highly successful African-
American entrepreneur and philanthropist who lived
from 1867 to 1919. When she was in her thirties, her
hair began to fall out. She tried to remedy the situation
using existing products, but nothing helped. Then in a
dream she received the ingredients and formula for a hair
concoction. She tried it on her scalp, and it worked beautifully. She then got into the cosmetic industry, becoming
so successful that she eventually built a factory and several training schools.

No doubt, these amazing people and many others like them
mastered the Law of Vision and Goals. They can visualize during
their waking moments and also as they sleep, with important
visions coming to them in their dreams. Whether they are
genetically predisposed to being able to visualize so powerfully,
or they developed the ability over time, or they just stumbled
across it, we may never know.

Rest assured, however, that anyone, including you and your
child, can practice visualizing. The more you practice, the better
you'll get at it. In time, it may even become second nature for
you. You don't have to be born with an amazing capacity to
envision. Each of us has at least a smidgeon of this capacity to
begin with, and that's enough to get started. Now both you and
your child need to practice and trust the process.

With the Law of Vision and Goals, you can:

- *See results before they happen*

- *Compare possible outcomes that could result from different courses of action*

- *See yourself starting, doing, and completing a project
even before you take the first step in the physical realm*

- *Build a bridge from your thoughts and desires to your goals*

- *Go from dreaming about a goal to actually reaching that desired goal.*

Remember, the clearer you can see it in your thoughts, the greater the chances are that you'll incorporate it into your life experiences. When you as a parent take the time to teach your child to visualize their goals in great detail, you will teach them how to psyche themselves up for having that experience on the Earth plane. You practice in your mind. And you build a bridge from today to the future of your desire.

Example: That Big Trip

Ever since she was a little girl, Jennifer wanted to travel to Japan. She'd been fascinated with the island nation from the moment a Japanese exchange student visited her fifth grade class and taught the kids how to create origami peace cranes, write Kanji characters, and do traditional dances. She wanted to travel there and see for herself the culture that had enchanted her so.

The problem was, she didn't have the means. She had just completed college with a liberal arts degree. Uncertain of her next move, Jennifer got a job as a waitress. It was a temporary gig, something she did so she could pay the rent and utilities and make her car payments, a way to support herself until she figured out her next step.

It wasn't just any restaurant that she worked at, though. It was a Japanese restaurant near her college, a popular place with students and faculty alike. While she worked there, she dreamed of her trip. She pictured herself in Japan, meeting people, learning more about the culture, learning the language. She also learned as much as she could from her co-workers, a couple who were born in Japan. Jennifer learned about the traditions. She learned

46

how to prepare Japanese dishes. She also picked up quite a bit of the language.

Meanwhile she never stopped picturing herself going to Japan. She visualized everything, from finding the airline tickets online to purchasing them, to flying across the Pacific and landing at Narita Airport, to taking the trains to get around in Tokyo and its surroundings, to meeting people and being immersed in the Japanese culture. She had no idea how this would come about, or when it would happen, but she never stopped daydreaming about it. She never stopped visualizing herself there. And she never doubted that it would one day happen.

The opportunity came out of the blue. One of her former professors came in to get a bite to eat and was happy to see Jennifer again. The two caught up on what they'd been doing since they'd last seen each other. When the professor learned of Jennifer's dream to visit Japan, he informed her of a new program on campus, a work exchange type of program. He gave her the contact information of the person running the program and wished her luck.

Jennifer's heart beat a mile a minute. She couldn't wait to end her shift and get home to call the head of the program. She felt a little disappointed when the voicemail message said she was out of the office, but would return the next day. Oh well, thought Jennifer I've waited this long for my Japan trip. I can wait a little longer to talk to this person.

The next day, first thing in the morning, Jennifer tried calling that number again. This time, the person was in! They agreed to meet later that day.

When they met, Jennifer grew even more excited. She learned that several schools in Japan were looking for American college graduates to live in Japan for one to two years and teach English to secondary school students. All that was needed was a four-year college degree, a high grade point average, and a willingness to live in Japan for a while. Jennifer had all three. Being proficient in the Japanese language wasn't even a requirement, since the goal was to immerse these students completely in an English-speaking environment. She was thrilled beyond measure.

She applied immediately. The waiting was the hardest part. Every day she went to work, and then rushed home to see if a call had come in. After three weeks, there was a message on her answering machine. She screamed with delight when she listened to it—she'd been accepted into the program! Jennifer was going to Japan. Her lifelong dream, which she had thought about, daydreamed about, and envisioned practically every day from the time she was a fifth grader, was coming true.

The Law At Work In Your Life

The Law makes sense, doesn't it? People have worded it in countless different ways, but whatever words are used, it works the same. You have to see it in your head first. You have to create the reality within you, and then it becomes reality outside of you. The better you see it, in great detail, the easier it becomes for you to manifest it. Seeing yourself achieving a particular goal creates a roadmap, a blueprint, an energy map that guides you along the way. Don't you agree that this would be a valuable lesson for all parents to teach their child?

That dream or goal of yours may be far off, but you must begin thinking of it before it can ever happen. The sooner you start to think about it and envision yourself doing it, the sooner you begin to align yourself with the successful execution and completion of that goal. Take a look at the Law of Vision and Goals once more:

What you see clearly in your thoughts is what you get in your life experiences. Visualize yourself achieving a goal, and you form a bridge to reaching that goal.

What type of bridge do you intend to build to get you from point A, where you are at this moment, to point B, where you wish to be? Can you see yourself taking the first step? What does that involve? What do you then see from the perspective of having completed the first step? Do you see yourself taking the second step? How does it feel to reach step two? What's the step you need to take after that? Can you see yourself taking it? Can you picture, in as much detail as possible, every step you'll be taking to get you to that desired point B?

Practice, practice, practice! Let the following six steps encourage you and your child both how to become a better visualizer and goal-getter:

1 Find a quiet moment in your day. Go outside, or to a quieter room in your home, if need be. While doing these exercises, be mindful when you are teaching your child to do these steps, not to overwhelm them. It's helpful with very young children to just ask them just one thing in their life they wish to accomplish.

2 Ask yourself, what do I wish to accomplish? It's completely up to you what you come up with. It could be short-term and immediate, such as getting to bed at a reasonable hour, or it could be something you'd like to do the next day, such as going to the nearby library or bookstore during lunch so that you can pick up a copy of that book you've wanted to read. It could also be a long-term goal, such as learning ballroom dancing. Get creative, and be honest with yourself.

3 Write down your goal. Then write down a step-by-step plan. For example, to get to bed at a reasonable hour, you might write down something like this:

- Finish drying the dishes

- Set out the kids' clothes for tomorrow

- Tuck the children into bed

- Read them a short bedtime story

- Brush your teeth

- Put on a relaxing CD

- Go to bed

- Fall asleep to relaxing music

A child's one goal may be as simple as getting to school on time. Whatever your goal may be, write out your step-by-step plan. Then help your child do the same.

4 Next, visualize what you just wrote. In your mind, see each step, one by one. Spend a few moments envisioning yourself doing exactly what you wrote. Visualize yourself through the entire sequence. Repeat this over a couple of times in your mind.

5 Pick a specific day and time to carry out your goal, if it's a shorter goal, or to begin working on your goal, if it's a longer one. It's best if you can get to it sooner than later. Mark it on your calendar. Give your child a calendar so that they can do the same. Let your child pick out their own calendar, one that's fun for them, that way they will want to look at it often. Why not add your goals to your "to do" list as well? Treat it like you would any other appointment posted on your calendar. Make a commitment to keep this very important appointment.

6 When the designated day and time arrives, carry out your goal (or for a long-term goal, carry out the first few steps you've outlined and visualized).

The point of these six steps is to get you and your child both into the practice of thinking, planning, visualizing, and attaining your goals. As we've said before, and we'll say again, the Law will serve you well. It's up to you to make the commitment to practice it. Once you do, you'll see that this Universal Law works beautifully. All you have to do is see it through, and the Law does the rest.

Affirmations To Use

As a Parent did you realize that your daydreams can be the springboard for creating a better life for you? In the exact same way that you daydream about spending time at the beach, talking to someone who interests you, or skipping work to go fishing, you can use the power of your mind to visualize your success and happiness. The Universal Law of Vision and Goals states that what you see clearly in your thoughts is what you get in your life experiences. Many times a child's goal will manifest faster than parents. Why? Because they have a better imagination then adults. You can learn a lot from your child on how to use your imaginations. When a child daydreams about something, they are really feeling it. Many of you as parents can visualize a dream, but can you really feel it? For instance when a child is pretending they are a movie star they really feel that they are a movie star. Watch your child and learn how to feel when you daydream like they do.

With that in mind, start visualizing yourself achieving a goal and really feel yourself attaining it. Pick a goal, any goal you like, and begin with it.

To help you in your practice of visualizing, we present here several affirmations for you and your child to use every day. The more you say them to yourself, the easier it will become for you to visualize the life experiences you wish to have. These affirmations will help the process of visualization become second nature for you. For added power, feel free to say them out loud. But even if you choose to say them quietly to yourself in your mind, trust that they will assist you in reaching your goal.

> **Affirmation 1:** My mind is a powerful, useful tool for creating pictures of the way I see myself. I use my mind to visualize myself the way I wish to be. Using my mind, I bring about the change that I want.

> **Affirmation 2:** My thoughts are clear. My thoughts are pure. My thoughts are worthy.

> **Affirmation 3:** I am a creative person. I create images in my mind of the life of my dreams. I visualize myself happy, successful, energetic, powerful, and complete.

> **Affirmation 4:** I shall make it my purpose to discover my goal.

> **Childs Affirmation:** I shall make my goals.

Exercises To Do With Your Child

Now it's time for you and your child to have some fun with the Law of Vision and Goals. These exercises will help you get more and more comfortable with this Universal Law. They'll also give you the practice that you need to become a master at visualizing and goal-attaining. Think of it as advanced training using basic principles.

1 **Grow Your Garden.** Prepare a small patch of your yard for growing fruits, vegetables, or flowers, whatever you choose, with your child. It could be a strawberry patch, or a row of tomatoes, or a cluster of pansies, anything you like. If you don't have a yard, then plant a mini

indoor garden. Pick a sunny spot by a window, get a pot that's just the right size for you, fill it with good soil, and get a few seeds from the store or from a gardening enthusiast friend.

Once you've prepared the soil for your indoor or out-door gardens, be it mini or larger, go ahead and plant the seeds with your child. Follow the instructions on your pack. Or consult with that gardening enthusiast and plant the seeds according to his or her instructions. Water your seeds gently.

Every day both of you tend to your gardens. And as you do, spend a few moments sitting next to it. Visualize the seeds growing into first tiny shoots that push out of the soil, and then baby plants, and later bigger and bigger plants. Visualize the flowers forming on the branches of each plant. Visualize the fruit start to form. Every day spend time seeing it in your mind first. Then, watch it happening in your garden. It's nothing short of miracu-lous! Don't be a bit surprised if your child's plants grow bigger and faster than yours. They tend to think outside the box, and put a lot more energy and love into this exercise. I for one have seen their plants grow twice as fast as their parents do. You could also make two small gardens. With the other one just plant the seeds and leave it to grow on its own. Then you both can compare the difference between the two gardens. When I did this with my own children I was shocked to see the difference.

2 **Create A List.** Write down a list of five items you plan to do today. Your child may want to start out with only two or three things on their list. Take into account the rest of your schedule, and make your list of five items do-able in light of the other things you need to accomplish today.

For each item on your list, spend a moment or two pic-turing yourself doing it. You don't need to spend much time picturing each, but do try to picture it as clearly and in as much detail as possible. See you start it, work on it, and complete it.

Keep your list handy. As the day moves on, complete each of the five items listed. You can do them all at once, or a couple in the morning, one in the afternoon, and a couple in the evening, whatever works best. When you complete an item cross it off the list before moving on to the next activity. Crossing it out gives you a little tangible reward, a feeling of, "Hey, I did it, Yea!"

3 **Take A Mini Class.** Ever wanted to try your hand at ethnic cuisine? Learning Sign language? Wine tasting? Or maybe even Scuba diving? Check with your local parks and recreation department to see what classes they offer. Or check with your nearby community college and ask for a schedule of the continuing education or personal enrichment courses they offer. It is always fun to find classes you and your child can do together. Try not to sign your child up for too many classes as they tend to get overwhelmed. One or two would be a great start. By the way, what's the worse thing that can happen when you take a class? You learn you didn't like the class, but the positive side of it is, you get to meet people in the class you might not have ever met had you not taken the class.

Once you get the schedule, look over the list of courses. Circle the ones that catch your eye. Then narrow down to one you'd like to take. Next, envision yourself going through the process: signing up for the class, getting the supplies and materials you'll need, attending class, participating in lectures and projects, doing the homework, and completing the class.

Make sure it's a class you or your child really wants to take. It doesn't have to be anything complicated or difficult, or even long—just fun for you. As you visualize

54

yourself in the class, feel your anticipation and excitement growing. Pump yourself up for it!

Then, take the class. Have a ball with it. Enjoy every moment. Learn as much as you can. And when you're done, enjoy the feeling of accomplishment that comes from completing your goal. Don't forget to tell your child how proud you are of them for taking the class.

Summing It Up

Visualization, which is the process of creating internal mental images to envision something that hasn't happened yet, is a powerful mental practice run.

Practice makes perfect, whether you or your child practice in the physical realm or in the mental domain.

Visualization is a very useful technique that enables one to "see" and "experience" results before they happen.

When you do a mental trial run, your mind works to program the cells of your body and imprint an energy pattern of a successful outcome into your psyche.

The more you visualize yourself achieving, in great detail, the more you prepare and program yourself for making this your reality.

The mechanisms of visualization and goal-setting can help each of us transform our lives from ordinary to extraordinary.

When you and your child take the time to visualize your goals in great detail, you will psych yourself out for having that experience on the Earth plane.

Being able to see yourself achieving a particular goal creates an energy map that guides you along the way.

You and your child CAN use the power of your mind to visualize your success and happiness.

Chapter Four

The Law Of Affirmation

"Success is a process, a quality of mind and way of being,
An outgoing affirmation of life."
— Alex Noble

Chapter 4

"Life is beautiful."

"You're awesome!"

"You can do it!"

All of these are beautiful affirmations. When you read each one, how did you feel? Did you feel elevated, built up in some way? Or perhaps even worthy, valuable, loved? Now read these affirmations to your child and ask them how it made them feel. Now go back and read each line again. Take your time. Savor each affirmation, internalize it, and own it. How does each phrase make you feel? I hope your answer is "good." Or better yet, "fantastic!" Say words back and forth to each other with your child, each time asking each other how that word made you feel. You can do this in the car, on a walk, even waiting at the doctor's office.

Words have great power. Whether it's the spoken word or the word that lives in your thoughts, a word can affect you greatly. It can keep you from reaching your heart's desire, or it can open the door to your most precious dreams. Which would you rather choose?

Some of us were lucky enough as children to have parents, grandparents, or other caring adults in our lives who lifted us up with their kind, loving words. Some of us did not have that growing up. If you longed to hear phrases like "I love you," or "I'm so proud of you," but you never did, you have my genuine compassion. The pain in your heart is real and justified.

But I want to tell you that you can start to take steps right now to ease that pain. Even if there was nobody there to give you affirmations as a child, and even if there is no one who affirms you today, YOU have the power to affirm yourself! You can take control of your self-worth by starting to validate the beautiful, creative, and amazing being you are. You are a miracle!

Trust me on this—regard yourself as the precious person and mighty spiritual being you truly are, and it will lift you up. Affirming yourself will give you more confidence, more self-worth, and greater self-respect. It will enable you to love yourself even when those around you do not know how to love.

Let's look at the fourth Universal Law:

The Law Of Affirmation: What you say is what you get. The words you say plant seeds in your soul that grow into manifestations in your life.

When you speak a word, or a phrase or sentence, you send a frequency out of your body and into the world. Every word has a frequency of sound associated with it, whether that word is "love," "fear," "like," "hate," "can," "can't," "impossible," or "possible." In addition, every word has an energy associated with it. Some of these "energies" emanate from the love realm, while others do not. For this reason, it is so important to watch our words carefully. What do we want ourselves and our children to send out into the world? What frequencies and energies are we creating with our mouths? Wise people are mindful of the words they release and the power that their words carry.

Let's experiment a little. Read the following phrases. Then ask yourself and your child this question: What energy might each one carry?

- *Floating clouds (energy of peace and relaxation)*

- *Ugly warts (energy of discord and dis-ease)*

- *Amazing discovery (energy of promise and excitement)*

- *Beautiful soul (energy of beauty and awe)*

- *Lazy slob (energy of disrespect and abuse)*

- *Wonderful universe (energy of wonder and greatness)*

- *Cozy home (energy of warmth and safety)*

If simple phrases can create such energies, imagine what whole sentences, even what entire conversations can do. And imagine what the thoughts running through your mind produce. Perhaps you are mindful of what you say to others. That is good and commendable. But how careful are you with the words you choose when you speak to yourself in your mind? We need to teach ourselves and children to be mindful of the words we speak because of the energy it carries. Once I asked a little girl named Lynn how these phrases made her feel. When I said lazy slob, she said it made her feel happy. Why? Because her mom told her men are lazy slobs and that women will own all the money in the world someday. Being a girl meant she would be rich when she grew up. Knowing how this little five year old girl perceives her moms words might make you as a parent even more mindful of the words you speak because you just never know how your own child will perceive them.

What Does This Mean For You?

Have you heard of a man named Dannion Brinkley? You may have read one or more of his books, or perhaps you've seen him on television or heard him on radio. He had a very dramatic experience in 1975: While talking on the telephone, he was struck by lightning and died. He was dead for 28 minutes before coming back to life.

During that half hour when his body was clinically dead, Dannion's spirit was visiting incredible heavenly realms. He visited an amazing city of light. He went through a life review, seeing every moment of his life flash before him in an instant. He met beings of light who shared with him the future direction of humanity. It was an incredible experience, to say the least.

After he returned to his body, Dannion needed years of rehabilitation. The lightning had damaged so much of his body that he needed time to heal and recover. With both patience and determination, he improved physically and was able to live a normal life again.

But something else happened. I have had the pleaser of talking to Dannion a few times and believe me when I tell you he NEVER expected to have the life he would live after having his near death experience. I am pretty sure he even fought talking about what went on during his near death experience for a while. The man he was before and the man he was after his near death experience were two totally different people. He came back a changed man in more ways than one. For one thing, he stopped being self-centered and began to actively help others. He does so much for others and the world now. He started to really think about how his words and actions affect others. He also noticed that he had come back with special powers he never had before. Dannion had returned with a intuitive awareness.

At first he didn't even realize it. After a while, he noticed that he knew what people were about to ask him even before they said anything. Once he recognized his highly attuned intuitive powers and learned to handle them better, he noticed something else. He could pick up people's moods and even felt bombarded by others' emotions (until he learned how to regulate his ability, turning it "off" when he needed to).

Until he learned how to work with his new awareness, though, he involuntarily picked up thoughts and feelings from friends and strangers alike. If Dannion went to the supermarket, for example, or even if he just looked out his window at people passing by, he'd automatically pick up on what they thought and how they felt. And wow, was he surprised by people's self-perceptions. In his bestseller, At Peace In The Light, Dannion stated:

"I was amazed by how negatively people viewed themselves. I still am. Beginning in those early days, it became clear to me that most people have a very low opinion of themselves. As I watched people go in and out of the store, I could hear their self-impressions. Most of their feelings were negative … they focused on the surface things in their lives and picked themselves apart. Person after person, I could hear them think that they were ugly, overweight, or poor, or bad parents, or just downright dumb."

(excerpt from At Peace In The Light, by Dannion Brinkley with Paul Perry)

What a sad state of affairs. The Law of Affirmation, "What you say is what you get," works regardless of what you say. If you tell yourself, in your mind or out loud, that you are not worthy, that's how you will live your life.

Thankfully, there is an antidote. It is the Law of Affirmation … used wisely. You can start to diminish your negative internal talk by consciously affirming yourself. After all, you are:

- *Magnificently created*
- *Remarkable in countless ways*
- *Skilled and talented*
- *Able and capable*
- *Dignified*
- *Powerful*
- *Creative*
- *Empowered*

Why focus on negatives (some of which are rather insignificant when compared to this list) when you can instead focus on these marvelous positives? Why "down yourself" when you can affirm yourself using words that describe you in all your shining glory?

There is no need to be hard on yourself or others. Practice saying kind words to yourself, your family, your friends, your pets. When you and your child release kind, gentle, and uplifting words, you release positive energy to go with the words you speak. Even plants respond positively to good vibes. Many people talk to their plants. This is nothing new. Throughout the ages, farmers and gardeners have talked to their plants, claiming that they grow better as a result. You or your child may have experienced these results yourself. A good way to experience this is to buy two plants. Place them in separate rooms. Talk to one and not the other and see the difference yourself of how the plant grows.

If plants can pick up your vibrations, you can be sure that people and animals can, and they will respond accordingly. It truly is wise to think before you speak. How will your words affect the recipient? With the words you are about to say, are you treating the other person the way you yourself wish to be treated? If not, then do not open your mouth yet. Take several deep breaths. Think of a positive thing to say in place of what you were about to say. Choose to utter the positive words instead.

Example: A Parent Learns

Joe was a good dad, but he was a little harsh. That's how he'd been raised, and he just didn't know any better. When his young children did well, he praised them exuberantly. But when they messed up, he was quick to intervene. Too often, though, he said things that he later regretted.

He had a boy, age 4, and a girl, age 2. They were cute, fun kids who got along well, played together nicely most of the time, and didn't cause too much trouble. Being a perfectionist, Joe expected perfection out of his children. He was fun to be around when the kids were in a good mood. He loved to play with them, read to them, and make up silly songs with them.

When the kids were cranky, or hungry, or tired, then Joe wasn't as much fun to be with. Not knowing what else to do, he belittled them. He'd tell his boy, "Why are you crying so much? You're not a baby anymore! Cut it out." Or he'd tell his girl, "Stop being a spoiled little princess. You get what you get. Don't bother me anymore!" He was harsh with his words.

The problem with this is that the children started to associate themselves with negative labels. The boy heard his father refer to him as a "baby." The girl heard her father refer to her as "spoiled." Children internalize what their parents say to them, and that's just what these two did.

Instead of the normally behaved children behaving better these two siblings starting acting up more. It was unintentional; it was merely a response to Joe's negative energy. The boy acted more like a "baby" and the girl acted more "spoiled." On top of it, their feelings were hurt. They didn't like getting insults from their dad. And in addition to that, they began to be afraid of their father. They liked being around him when he was in a good mood, but in the back of their mind, they began to hold the question, "When's he going to blow up?" This sense of fear created an emotional distance between the children and their father.

Meanwhile, Joe's in-laws were seeing exactly what was happening. Knowing that they couldn't just tell their son-in-law that he needed to change—they didn't want to sound like they were criticizing his parenting approach—they instead gave a gift to their daughter and son-in-law: a positive parenting book.

Because it was written by a popular parenting expert, Joe and his wife agreed to read it.

Thankfully Joe was open-minded enough to realize, from reading this book, that he was harming his young kids every time he got angry with them. He began to see that love and patience work better in the long run. Being a practical sort of guy, he was willing to do a little experimenting himself. He spent a week doing what he'd been doing thus far, and he carefully observed his kids' reactions. He noticed that when he yelled or derided them, they became withdrawn. He could see the hurt in their eyes, and that hurt him.

He then tried the approaches he'd read about in his new book. Joe used only uplifting words. When the kids acted up, he counted to five or ten to calm himself down. Then he intervened, firmly but gently. Either he removed the toy that was causing the trouble, or he separated the children. He did what he needed to do to resolve the situation and keep the peace. But he refrained from insulting his children. He refrained from using negative labels, as he'd been doing before.

Joe then observed his children. He noticed that they cried less, fought less, and acted up less when he was gentler with them. Best of all, they did not withdraw from him, and the hurt was no longer in their eyes. He realized that he had come across very sound parenting advice in that book. Joe opted to continue with his new approach of parenting without resorting to put-downs. From that point forward he chose his words carefully. He selected life-affirming words. As a result, his relationship with his kids improved greatly, as did their self-esteem.

The Law At Work In Your Life

Have you heard this little schoolyard rhyme?

"Sticks and stones may break my bones, but words will never hurt me."

If only that statement were true. You'd have to be awfully thick-skinned for this to be true. In reality, words do hurt us. We may wish that they wouldn't, but they do. It hurts to be insulted. It hurts to be bad-mouthed. It hurts to be lied about, rumored about, and misrepresented. It hurts.

Knowing this, what can you do? Well, the Law of Affirmation works both ways. Words can hurt, but words can also help. They can heal. They can soothe. They can uplift. They can affirm. What do you choose to do with your words?

Look once more at this Universal Law:

What you say is what you get. The words you say plant seeds in your soul that grow into manifestations in your life.

This is eye-opening, isn't it? "What you say is what you get." The words don't just go "out there." They affect YOU. When you insult someone else, you hurt yourself. Much like Joe in our previous example was unintentionally hurting his little kids. Whenever he insulted his children, he drove them further away from himself. He hurt his relationship with them. He hurt himself.

Knowing that words said to hurt someone else come right back and hurt you, why would you ever choose to utter such words? It is infinitely better, for you and for your loved ones, to send out words that will be of genuine service to the recipient. That which you send out comes right back to you, in some way, at some point.

Even when you're at the grocery store, your reaction to others makes a difference, to them and to you. Even the simplest gift—a smile, a nod, a "hello"—can make both you and the recipient feel good and worthy. Try it! And ask your child to do the same.

And be sure to try these six steps with your child. So you can better understand and embrace the Law of Affirmation:

1 You and your child write down seven phrases you would love to hear someone say to you (with a young child one to three will do depending on their age). Ideas include: You did a great job. I appreciate your many qualities. Thank you for helping me. Or anything else of your choosing.

2 In the next week or two, you and your child select three different people. Each person will receive one or two of the affirmations you wrote down in Step 1. You can deliver your affirmation in person, over the phone, or by email, but you'll make the best connection and perhaps have the greatest impact in person. So choose to deliver your affirmation in person where possible, and use the other methods when this is not possible (such as in the case of a person living far away). You as a parent will find the people your child chooses to do this for enlightening. One child I know named Michael chose a crabby old man that did not want children walking on his lawn. When I asked him why, he said that he felt this man needed it more than people he loved. Guess what? The man and he are now great friends.

3 After you have delivered your positive words to each of these three people, then you and your child affirm yourselves. Stand in front of a mirror. Don't worry about how you look. It's OK if your hair's a little messy, or you're not wearing makeup, or you haven't shaved. No problem. Just look straight into your reflected eyes, and repeat the seven affirmations from Step 1 to yourself. Say them boldly, with confidence. Mean them. You may have to write them down for your child to read or have them repeat it after you if they are a young child.

4 Visualize the universe affirming you. Using a child's imagi-nation, have each beautiful element of the universe come say "hello" to you and tell you that you're special. Close your eyes, and in your mind let the stars come down to greet you. Watch a rainbow stretch out to meet you. Imagine the sun's rays racing forth to be the first to say hello to you in the morning. Picture every flower and tree saying "hi" as you pass by them. I am always amazed at how good children are at doing this. We can learn from them doing this exercise.

5 Now both you and your child spend a day smiling. Smile at your reflection in the mirror. Smile at everyone you pass. Some people may smile back. Others may look away in discomfort. That's OK. It's their choice. You and your child have done your part. You have affirmed your-self and others through your smiles. I am amazed at how many people look away from me when I do this. But they never seem to look away from children!

6 Both you and your child start to share compliments with a pet, a plant, or each other every day. A child can even pick a favorite stuffed animal, to practice giving compli-ments to. Ok, if no one is looking you can even buy your own stuffed animal to give compliments to. Give your animal or plant friend, or your fluffy inanimate object, a genuine compliment. I give each of my animals a compli-ment every day. That's a lot of compliments as I have 8 cats, two dogs, and a bunny. Plus I give the birds, deer and even the flowers at my house compliments.

The beauty of saying kind, positive words is that the benefit is twofold. Your recipient is showered by a healthy dose of positive energy, and at the same time, positive energy spreads within yourself. When you affirm another, you affirm yourself. It's that basic and that powerful.

Affirmations To Use

Words have power. So why not use powerful words that will affirm you? You and your child deserve to hear praise on a daily basis. You truly are a precious child of the universe, a wonderful and complete person, a beautiful expression of Spirit. With the Universal Law of Affirmation, what you say is what you get. So why don't you and you child both remember to give yourselves the gift of kindness, support, and love by saying powerful words, each and every day? That way you will affirm who you are, in all of your awesomeness!

Affirmation 1: I like who I am. I have gifts and abilities given to me which I value.

Affirmation 2: I give and receive from the heart.

Affirmation 3: I am whole. I am well. I am of service to others. I am important. I am valuable. I matter.

Affirmation 4: All is well in my world, because it's my world and I choose it to be.

Child s Affirmation: All is well with my Life.

Some people find that it's helpful to get into a trance-like state when saying an affirmation. In this way we are most receptive to the words and they can make the greatest impact. Being in a trance-like, or a meditative, state will allow us to absorb what we say better, internalizing the thoughts and ideas conveyed by the affirmations more fully.

One way to get into a trance-like state is to repeat a phrase or an affirmation over and over again. For example, take a look at affirmation #2. By repeating these words, you can get yourself into a focused, meditative state. Rhythmic breathing also helps. For example, breathe in with the word "give," and breathe out on the word "receive." Practice with just these two words first.

Breathe in and say Give. Breathe out and say Receive. Then switch the words around. Breathe in with the word Receive. Breathe out with the word Give. Ok, don't try this too fast and make yourself pass out. Take it nice and slow.

Exercises To Do With Your Child

What's in a word? Remember the little girl named Lynn and what she felt when she heard the word lazy slob? Perhaps a word is a lot more than you realized, as you discovered in this chapter. Words are powerful. Words carry weight. Words can hurt, or they can heal. Choose to use your words to heal. Begin with yourself. Once you've healed yourself, you are in a position to help heal others. And then, you can begin to heal the rest of the world. As always, take it one step at a time. Try the following exercises with your child to affirm yourself using the power of words. Remember to do these exercises in accordance with your child's age and ability. You may have to ask a very young child what they wish you to write out for them.

1 **Write A Love Story.** This is a great way for you and your child to get to know each other better. You could even write the love story to each other.

Using the following words, write a story. Make it as long or as short as you wish. Just make sure it is a "love story." Not a romance necessarily, but a story about LOVE, as in the unconditional love the universe has for each of us, or the love we share for one another as human beings. Here are the words to use:

Love, peace, joy, like, sunshine, goodness, grace, positive, river, accept, majestic, laugh, fun, smile, song, together, best, clear, nice, dear, excellent, great, happy, interesting, kind, life. Why not let your child make up their own words here?

After you've written your love story, both you and your child should read it aloud, either to yourself, each other or to a special someone who will understand and appreciate your beautiful words. Or read it to your beloved pet.

2 **Dictionary Search.** You and your child can peruse through a dictionary. Ignore any negative words you might encounter. Instead, make a list of all the positive, beautiful words you find. Once your list is finished, review it. Circle your five favorite ones. Use each one to describe something about yourself. A fun way to do this exercise with your child is to ask them to look through one of their favorite books and circle the words that make them feel good.

For example, if you chose "joyful" as one of your favorite words, then you may write something like this: "I am joyful when I smile at the world." A child's word may be as simple as happy. They could write or if they are very young you could write something like this, "I am happy when I pet my kitty."

3 **Jump**. Now you and your child should jump. Yes, you read correctly, jump! But jump only if you are physically able to, of course. You can jump in place, or jump rope, or if you have a mini trampoline, use that. Perhaps you'd like to do jumping jacks. Your child will love to do this one with you as they tend to have mastered the art of jumping. Doing this exercise has a bonus…it helps you stay in shape.

Every time you jump, shout out an adjective that describes yourself, such as special, generous, compassionate, trustworthy, unique. A young child may use words like happy, smart, and pretty, or even brave. When you get tired, stop. When you feel your energy's back, jump again, shouting out other marvelous adjectives that describe you in all your glory! Trust me when I tell you that your child will want to wear you out doing this exercise. But I found that many very young children will take a LONG nap after doing this fun jumping.

Summing It Up

Words have great power. Whether it's the spoken word or the word that lives in your thoughts, a word can affect you greatly.

Even if nobody affirmed you when you were a child, and even if no one affirms you today, you have the power to affirm yourself. And teach your child to do the same.

When you and your child learn to affirm yourselves it gives you more confidence, more self-worth, and greater self-respect.

You and your child both must be mindful of what you say to others and of what you speak to yourself in your mind.

You and your child will start to diminish your negative internal talk by consciously affirming yourself.

When you and your child say kind, gentle, and uplifting words, you release positive energy to go with the words you speak.

That which you send out comes right back to you, in some way, at some point.

When you affirm another, you affirm yourself.

Chapter Five

The Law Of Attraction

"If you have zest and enthusiasm you attract zest and enthusiasm. Life does give back in kind."
— Norman Vincent Peale

Chapter 5

On the outside, David and Mike lived very different lives. One was viewed as successful by society; the other was not. David was a CPA working for a large firm in California. He had known success his whole life, first in high school as valedictorian, then in college with several scholarships that paid his way, and now in the world of business, where his reputation as an outstanding CPA was known well in his company.

Mike, on the other hand, knew the California prison system quite well. He dropped out of high school during his junior year, got into gang activity and drug dealing, and has been in and out of prison for the last decade, from the time he was 19. While these two guys live very different lives, both have one thing in common: they're miserable.

David is tired of the predictability of his life. Whereas business and the thought of working for a high-profile firm once excited him, it now bores him. Company meetings and company parties are dull and dreary events. He finds many of his fellow workers and bosses to be shallow. David feels stuck, and he doesn't know how to get out of the rut he's in. He longs for a life of travel, more excitement, and more interesting people. He's looking for a greater purpose to his life. He wants to do something that matters.

Meanwhile, Mike is sick of his life of crime. He's tired of the prison inmates and just as tired of the so-called "friends" he has on the outside. He feels his life is headed nowhere. Mike feels like an aimless drifter and wants more direction and stability in his life. He wants greater purpose to his life. He wants to meet people who are healthy and are making positive contributions to society. He desperately wants to change.

What neither David nor Mike realizes is this: They are living only half of the Law of Attraction. This is the whole Law:

The Universal Law of Attraction: Like attracts like. Be the person you want to be to attract the people you want to meet, the experiences you wish to have, and the possessions you seek to enjoy.

The only part of the Law they're living is this: Like attracts like. David has become a predictable, reliable worker in a large corporation. He's loyal and responsible, which are good traits, but he's also become dull, conventional, too consistent. He takes few risks and doesn't venture out of his comfort zone. As a result, he attracts people and circumstances that are much like him: predictable, traditional, boring. There's nothing spontaneous, adventurous, or exciting in his life because there's nothing spontaneous, adventurous, or exciting about him anymore. Because remember: Likes do attract like.

Likewise, Mike with his life of crime, regularly lies, cheats, swindles, and steals. He's become untrustworthy and downright dangerous. As a result, the people he attracts into his life share these characteristics. They make a living cheating, lying, stealing, and swindling. By his behavior, Mike "invites" risky, life-threatening scenarios into his life every single day.

Both men lead very different lives, yet both feel completely trapped. They want out. They want a change. The problem is, they have no clue how to get themselves out of the prison they've created for themselves.

Here's where the second half of the Law comes in:

Be the person you want to be to attract the people you want to meet, the experiences you wish to have, and the possessions you seek to enjoy.

Until David and Mike learn to change themselves, they will not be able to attract to their lives what they so desire. It all starts on the inside. If Mike wants to attract more reliable people into his life, he first needs to become reliable himself. In many ways he needs to start over, learning how to be a responsible, trustworthy member of society. If David wants to have more exciting people in his life, then he first needs to become more exciting himself—by daring to take that trip to Tahiti, or enroll in that wine tasting class, or follow an interest he's truly passionate about. He needs to be willing to leave his comfort zone to find his passion.

Granted, neither of these two men is going to change overnight. Lasting transformation starts with small steps. The trick is to have the courage to start somewhere. Far too often, we become so accustomed to our way of life that we forget that there are other options. Once in a while, it's good to step back, look at the bigger picture of our existence, and ask ourselves: Are we moving in the right direction?

What Does This Mean For You?

As A Parent Do you feel stuck or trapped, as David and Mike do? If so, it's time to evaluate what you are "putting out" to see the great connection between what you are giving and what you are "getting back." Let's start with a few questions to ask yourself. You have to know your own self first, before you can help your child know themselves.

- *Do you find any aspect of your work rewarding?*

- *Are you doing what you want to do in life, or what you believe you should be doing?*

- *How do you greet others, both friends and strangers?*

- *What's the first thing you notice about another person?*

79

• *What do you do for fun?*

• *What is one of your favorite possessions, and why is it important to you?*

All right, let's look at each question individually now that you've had the chance to think about your answers. For the first question:

Do you find any aspect of your work or life rewarding?

. . . Well what did you answer? If your answer was "yes," good for you. You are doing something you enjoy, at least part of the time. And by doing what you enjoy, you're sending out positive vibrations along these lines: I like this. I'm having fun. I enjoy being here. As these positive vibes go out, you will attract people and situations that resonate with these concepts. People will appear who enjoy what they're doing, who are having fun and who truly like their work or vocation. By having a positive attitude yourself, you'll be open to those around you with a positive attitude.

If instead your answer to the question is "no," then you are sending a different message out there. You are saying, in effect, I don't like what I'm doing. I don't want to be here. This is no fun. And that "I don't like" and "I don't want" energy is going to come right back to you, bringing to you drudgery and heaviness, toil and worry, as well as people who are real downers. Watch what you put out. It will come back to you.

If you're not happy with your line of work, or the school you go to or even your life then make a change. You do not have to be "stuck." You have the power to get yourself "unstuck." No one else will do this for you. Start sharpening your resume. Begin looking through the online classifieds. Start talking to people who you know to see what else is out there. Evaluate your current interests, abilities, and desires, and then take action. You have the power to attract work that you enjoy!

On to the second question:

Are you really doing what you want to do in life, or what you believe you should be doing?

If you answered "want," again, that's good for you! You're creating synergy and certain energies of excitement and possibilities. If you answered "should," then I have a question for you: Why are you short-changing yourself? If you feel you are not enjoying your work, move aside—give someone else the opportunity to do it. Meanwhile, follow your passion. This is how you'll ultimately succeed in attracting to you the people, the experiences, and the possessions you want in your life.

Now the third question:

How do you greet others, both friends and strangers? Then take the time to notice how your child greets others.

Do you smile warmly? Do they? Do you make eye contact? Do they? Do you acknowledge the other person's presence? Do they or do you both tend to look away, look at the floor, or look beyond the person as if he or she were invisible? How you regard others is how they'll regard you. If you want people to connect with you, then you must make the effort to connect with them. If you want people to genuinely notice you, then you must first notice them. Remember Like attracts Like. You and your child should start to practice looking into peoples eyes when you talk to them. Ask your child to look at you when they are talking to you. Teach them that by doing this you are saying I value you, and I am giving you my attention when I talk to you.

The fourth question:

What's the first thing you or you child tend to notice about another person?

I find that children come up with quite different answers to this one. Many times they tend to notice the good qualities they have within themselves in others.

This is a very important question, because it'll give you many clues regarding where you are in your spiritual evolution. Do you first notice their flaws—rumpled clothes, messy hair, poor complexion, overweight, underweight, things of this nature? If so, then turn the tables around. What do you think others will first notice when they look at you?

Or do you first notice something beautiful about the other person, such as their friendly eyes, their radiant smile, their pretty hair, their nice hands, or their beautiful aura? If you choose to see the beauty in the other person before even noticing so-called flaws, then you're on the right track. You can see the exquisite spirit and accept the human shortcomings. May others greet you with that same level of grace! Teach your child to always look for the good qualities in someone. It's good to teach them about giving others a compliment. Like you have a nice coat, you have a nice smile, or your hair looks nice today. You and your child should practice the act of giving each other one compliment each day. This will get your child in the habit of giving out compliments.

Question number five:

What do you do for fun? Ok, children seem to always have great answers for this one. I guess adults have a lot to learn from children here also.

This question is also important, because it reveals your understanding of yourself, your compassion for and recognition of others, and again, your spiritual life progression. If you feel that addictive behavior—such as drinking, drug use, gambling, and so on—is fun, then you are presently stuck.

If this is the case, it is time to liberate you. Go to a 12-step program. Then really stick with the program, and complete it. That is a fantastic start. Then you will experience a wonderful liberation. You will be free to have real fun, not phony, addictive, so-called fun.

What is real fun? It is that which brings you joy without hurting yourself or another person. You and your child should make a list of fun things to do. It could be getting together with family and friends and watching a funny movie. Or maybe it's riding your bike on a path that meanders through a tree-filled park. It could be enjoying a hobby, like star-gazing or creating stained glass windows. Fun for you could be dinner out with friends, skiing every weekend, riding horses, playing computer games, traveling to Renaissance fairs, writing short stories, emailing pen pals, a night of dancing, building model rockets, sailing, or swimming with dolphins. The list is endless! Why not take your child's list of what they would like to do for fun, then do it with them. I assure you that if you open up your mind and heart to doing the fun things your child likes to do. YOU WILL HAVE FUN!

Double-check your list of what you find fun. I don't feel that young children have to do this exercise as they seem to be masters of having fun. If you're not happy with what you wrote down on your list, then take the time to evaluate yourself. Why do you find this activity fun? Why does that bother you? How would you feel if you freed yourself from this particular activity and found another one to occupy your time and energy? What steps can you take today to move away from the activity you wish to distance yourself from? What other things can you do instead for fun that might be more productive, more constructive, or healthier? Once again let your child lead you here. You may be pleasantly surprised at the insight they have to offer.

And now, the last question:

Ask yourself and your child what one of your favorite possessions is, and then ask why is it important to you or them?

I'll let you think about this one. You can figure it out on your own. But let me give you some replies I've heard others say:

"My computer, because I'm a writer and my computer allows me to write and get creative."

"My phone, because I use it to call my friends and family."

"My collection of books, because I love to read."

"My truck because I use it to take my friends and me camping, fishing, rafting, and hiking."

"My scroll saw, because I spend all my free time creating one-of-a-kind gifts and toys for friends, family, and customers."

What are you and your child's answers? Whatever it may be, it will speak volumes to you about what's important in your life. It will help show you who you are, right now. If you are happy with who you presently are, fantastic! If you're not pleased with your answer, then be glad you did this exercise. You now know more about yourself, and this will help you get "unstuck." Knowledge is power. Learning as much as you can about yourself will be the key to help you make the necessary modifications to gradually become the person you really want to be.

The way your child answers these question will teach you a lot about your child. I will also tend to bet that your child has a better understanding about who and what they want to be than you might have.

Example: Something's Out Of Sync

James had built a highly successful computer services business. He and his staff did it all, from designing websites to developing business graphics and logos to web hosting to computer trouble-shooting. With his electrical engineering and computer science undergraduate degree and his MBA from MIT, he had a winning combination. James was sharp, personable, and brilliant in both the technical and business aspects of his company, which had grown so quickly that he had to expand, opening several different divisions and putting competent people in charge of each.

Clients from all over the world liked his company's creative solutions, as well as the excellent customer service offered. Each employee, from the highest management levels to entry-level, was trained to be courteous and respectful when dealing with clients, whether they were customers, vendors, or potential business partners. His business quickly got a reputation for excellence.

It surprised James, then, when one of his divisions, the one that specialized in business graphics and logos, started to show signs of trouble. That division wasn't doing as well financially as all of the other divisions. In addition, customer complaints were starting to come in, and they appeared to be increasing. James decided to fly out to this particular division of his company and investigate.

He spent several days watching how business was conducted, as well as attending both formal and informal meetings. He took the time to talk with several employees from all levels and different departments. Slowly, a picture began to emerge, and it all pointed to the director of that division. It became clear that he wasn't following company policy that had made James' business stand out above the crowd. He was following his own agenda.

As a result of this director's "negative" management, the division was going down the tubes. His negative energy attracted more negative energy. Morale was low among employees. Customer service was poor. Vendors didn't want to stop by and deal with this division. Yes, like was attracting like.

James made the difficult decision of letting this director go. And he made sure to replace him with another director who was completely in line with the company culture of courtesy in all interactions, respect for every individual, top-notch service, commitment to personal and professional excellence, and creative solutions. Thankfully, that division turned around. Because the new director was aligned with the company goals and exuded positive energy, the division attracted positive people, positive vendors, and positive business partnerships. Morale improved, and quality improved. Again, like does attract like, in business and everywhere.

The Law At Work In Your Life

Have you seen the film "The Secret," or read the book by the same name? If not, you've probably heard of it nonetheless, as it's become quite popular throughout the world. It was written by an Australian television producer named Rhonda Byrne, with input from numerous spiritual gurus. It's a fun movie to watch, and the presentation is quite clever and entertaining. I myself watch it at least once a week. At the core of "The Secret" is the real jewel, though; it's all about The Law of Attraction, which Rhonda and others feel is the most powerful Law in the universe. I feel you must learn to use all the Universal Laws to be in balance in your life.

The "secret," then, is that like attracts like. You attract to yourself and to your life the people, circumstances, situations, opportunities, and "things" based on how you feel and what you think. Now, how would you benefit by putting this secret to work in your life? Would you watch what you say and think more carefully?

Look at the Law of Attraction once more:

Like attracts like. Be the person you want to be to attract the people you want to meet, the experiences you wish to have, and the possessions you seek to enjoy.

Now, compare and contrast the following statements with your child. And ask each other which statement from each pair would serve you better: Have fun with this and then you and your child both take the time to make up some of your own statements.

I'll never have a boyfriend/girlfriend.
OR
I'm excited by the possibility of meeting wonderful new people.

I'm no good at school.
OR
I enjoy learning new things.

I can't cook.
OR
I have fun dancing while I cook.

I'm no good at anything.
OR
I really enjoy trying new things.

Quite a difference between each statement, isn't there? Go a little deeper now and ask both yourself and child what might you attract from each statement? It's fairly obvious which thought will serve you better. Your job now is to train your-selves to think the thoughts that will attract to you only the things which you desire.

Not only think these thoughts, but feel them in every fiber of your being. Your thoughts and your feelings carry with them energy. You and your child will then both create this positive energy by what you are thinking and by how you are feeling. These steps will help you practice the Law of Attraction:

1 Go on an adventure with your child to look for good
news. Get on the Internet and start to look for good
events that are happening in the world. Make it a point to
ask your child each day to tell you things that happened
during their day that made them feel happy.

Expose your minds to good news, and it will help attract
good news to you.

2 Teach your child how to fill both your minds with all
good and beautiful things. You can do this by meditating
on a specific word, such as "love" or "peace." Or you can
do this consciously, by choosing what you read, what you
watch, and what you hear very selectively.

If the lyrics of the music you listen to offend or enrage,
switch to other music. If the book you're reading is disturb-
ingly graphic, move on to another book. There are plenty
out there to choose from. Teach your child to choose movies
that will lift their spirit rather than upset their mind.

By you choosing to teach your child and yourself what
to feed your minds and your emotions, you will have
much better control over what situations you attract to
your life. The choice, as always, is yours. Remember it is
always choice not chance that creates your destiny.

3 Take a moment with your child and picture in your mind
that which you'd like to attract into your lives. Is it more
friends? More sincere friends? Is it more money? More
free time? More meaningful work? Or even a new pet?

Whatever it is, both of you picture it clearly in your
mind. Hold that thought for a length of time. Immerse
yourself in that thought. Feel the feelings that arise based
on that thought. Enjoy the feelings.

4 Next, you and you child should come up with three steps you plan to take to make the picture in your mind from Step 3 happen. For example, to attract more sincere friends, will you take steps to be a sincere friend? This includes being sincere with yourself.

If you want to attract more free time, will you take steps to finish your work faster and more efficiently, lighten your load a bit, and remove distractions that might be wasting your time? Do your part first by picturing it in your mind, and then following it up with action.

5 You can choose with your child an uplifting movie to watch. Go to the theater, or rent a movie and bring it home. The requirement is that it has to be positive and uplifting. Something along the lines of "The Little Princess" (don't let the title turn you off, it's a beautiful movie with empowering messages throughout). Or "Forest Gump." Or the classic "It's A Wonderful Life" with Jimmy Stewart.

6 Learn with your child to practice courtesy. The more polite, courteous, and attentive you are to others, the more you'll receive courtesy and attention.

An important thing to remember as you and your child start to put the Law of Attraction into practice is that there's no room for manipulation. You are not trying to manipulate others here, as in being nice just so they can be nice to you. There's an element of phoniness to this approach, and people will ultimately see through that. This Universal Law, as all others, works on the genuine vibes you put out. So keep it real. Keep it genuine. You can never "trick" laws into working for you. They'll work if you play fairly and honestly.

Affirmations To Use

The Universal Law of Attraction is simple: like attracts like. But this statement holds profound meanings. The following affirmations can help you and your child use this powerful Law to your advantage. Commit them to memory, if you like. Say them anytime, anywhere. You and your child can start off each day with a few of them, or utter them to yourself in the shower. Review them during your lunch break. Say them to yourself at night before you go to bed. The more you review them, and the more you say them, the more that they'll become a part of you. Don't forget to help your young child make up affirmations that are easy for them to say and appropriate for their age.

> **Affirmation 1:** Because like attracts like, I will watch who I am and who I become carefully so that I may attract the people I wish to be like, and the circumstances I wish to experience.

> **Affirmation 2:** To have people around me who are interesting, kind, joyous, heart-centered, fun, and genuine, I will be interesting, kind, joyous, heart-centered, fun, and genuine.

> **Affirmation 3:** I understand that I attract circumstances and situations to myself. I strive to attract the circumstance and situations that will bring the highest good.

> **Affirmation 4:** The Law of Attraction is simple and profound. To attract laughter, I must laugh with people. To attract joy, I must cultivate a joyful heart. To attract peace, I must be at peace. To attract prosperity, I must adopt a frame of mind of abundance. To attract love, I must love.

> **Childs Affirmation:** I will only attract good things to me.

Is there anything else you'd like to add? As always, feel free to design your own affirmations. Your child or you may wish to address a very specific situation in your life. Or you may wish to uplift yourself in a way that gives you extra strength in one specific area. Remember to have fun with your affirmations, keep them positive, and personalize them whenever you desire to.

Exercises To Try With Your Child

It's exciting to think that you and your child can attract to yourselves what you want! Yes, you can have wonderful people around you. Yes, you can fill your days with rewarding work. Yes, you can have enough money to pay the bills and have a little left over for an occasional treat. You CAN! Like attracts like, so start being who you want to be in order to attract what you want in your life. Here are ideas to help you and your child practice the Law of Attraction:

1 **Dance!** Why? Because dancing gets your body parts to move and your circulation going. Dancing releases natural chemicals in your body that make you feel good. And dancing is a fun, healthy way to express yourself. I sing my affirmations while I dance. Try it, it's fun. Dance with your child and ask them how it makes them feel. Make up silly dance moves to try with each other. Yes, there is a bonus to this exercise also, it helps you stay in shape, and it tires very young children out. Often making them want to take a long nap!

When you dance, you release positive energy. You elevate yourself to a higher realm emotionally. You stimulate your brain to fire off positive thoughts and images. You put yourself in a better place. Why not try dancing outside in a soft rain, on a summer's day. This is sure to make you and your child giggle.

And through the Law of Attraction, what happens when you're thinking, feeling, and emitting positive vibrations? You attract "like," namely, positive vibrations. What a fantastic way to bring good energy to you and your child.

2 **Get Busy In The Kitchen with your child.** Whether you feel like creating a recipe from scratch, or you follow instructions from your favorite cookbook, try creating some positive energy in your kitchen. Schedule some time to cook. And as you prepare your feast, put love into your food. With every ingredient you add, think loving thoughts. Ask your child to send make believe kisses into the food and watch them smile, I bet who ever eats the food WILL feel the energy of those kisses. Play music while you're cooking. Dance while you're cooking. Feel yourself presenting the most exquisite gift with every ingredient you add. Feel the gratitude in your heart for your energy, your creativity, and this bountiful meal. Why not let your child feed their pets with the same positive energy? Let them pick out a colorful food bowl or placemat for their beloved pet. The bonus of doing this will be is that it makes the responsibility of taking care of a pet fun for a child. I know a friend who even found a recipe to make homemade dog biscuits to share with their dogs named Scooter and Snuggles. She has great fun making them with her children. And yes, they always make extra to give to their friends who have dogs. I myself grow catnip in my yard to share with my own cats, and to give to my friends who have cats.

Whether you choose to share your culinary creation with friends or family, or even a four legged pet, make eating it for yourself or four legged friend just as special as creating it. Set out nice dishes, glasses, and utensils, Use cloth napkins. Even when my friend's child gives their dogs a homemade dog biscuit she places it on a colorful doggie placemat. So why not let your child help you pick out a color theme for the food. Like red or blue napkins and ask them how that color makes them feel. Add a little vase with a flower, or light a candle. Enjoy this meal as though it was a celebration even if it's not a holiday or a so-called "special event." Remember that life is a celebration. The truth is, you have it within your power to make any meal, any day, any event, and any given moment special.

3 Call A Friend You Admire or do random acts of kindness. Do you have a friend who is extraordinary, someone who is gracious, kind, forgiving, and good-hearted? Call that friend just to say hello. Let your child do the same. When you reach out and connect to people you esteem, people who make you feel good inside, then you are bringing to yourself a little of that positive energy they emit. Take time to do random acts of kindness. Like, pay for a stranger's lunch or for the car wash for the person behind you. Buy fresh flowers and let your child give one to people everywhere you go. Let them feel the joy that comes back to them from the smiles of the people they give them to. Even a teller at the bank would love a flower. What you give out ALWAYS comes back to you.

Summing Jt Up

When we become so accustomed to our way of life that we forget there are other options, it's good to step back, look at the bigger picture of our existence, and ask ourselves: Are we moving in the right direction?

By having a positive attitude, you'll be open to those around you with a positive attitude.

You and your child should both remember to follow your passion. This is how you'll ultimately succeed in attracting to you the people, the experiences, and the possessions you want in your life.

If you want people to connect with you, then you must make the effort to connect with them.

Learning as much as you can about yourself, then helping your child do the same, will help you both make the necessary modifications to gradually become the people you really want to be.

You attract to yourself and to your life the people, circumstances, situations, opportunities, and "things" based on how you feel and what you think.

Train yourself to think the thoughts that will attract to you the things that you desire.

Feel these thoughts in every fiber of your being. Your thoughts and your feelings carry with them energy. You create this energy by what you think and by how you feel.

The choice of how you feel is always up to you and your child. No one can ever take that away from you.

Chapter Six

The Law Of
Focus and Discipline

"It's not what's happening to you now or what has happened in your past that determines who you become. Rather, it's your decisions about what to focus on, what things mean to you, and what you're going to do about them that will determine your ultimate destiny."
— Anthony Robbins

Chapter 6

T homas wants to take college classes. He works hard at a minimum-wage job, but he feels disappointed at the end of every month because after paying rent, making car payments, buying groceries, and taking care of all his other expenses, he has no money left over for his savings account. No money means no college classes.

He has his heart in the right place. He has wonderful goals; a talented artist, Thomas wants to take community college classes in web design and computer art so he can start a business creating websites. He dreams about this practically every day. Unfortunately, he's doing absolutely nothing to bring his beautiful dream closer to reality.

When he comes home from work each evening, he switches his TV on and watches several hours of mindless shows to unwind. He microwaves a meal and eats it in front of the TV. Then he gets on the Internet and spends another hour or so in chat rooms. He finishes, turns the computer off, and checks to see if he has any clean clothes to wear the next day. If not, he does a load of laundry. He prepares a sack lunch to take to work with him, and then gets on the phone to talk to his buddies. Finally, exhausted, Thomas heads to bed to get som e rest before having to get up early and go to work in the morning.

There is nothing wrong with watching TV, talking with friends, or going to chat rooms, if this truly makes Thomas happy. But what's wrong with this picture is that it does not, in fact, make him happy. These are simply activities he does to fill up his evenings. None of it is bringing him closer to his dream, which at this point is little more than a daydream. With his dream so far out of reach, he feels unfulfilled.

Thomas believes he won't be happy until he first takes college classes to learn how to design websites and then starts earning an income creating sites. While this is his desire, it is not his focus. He chooses to focus his time and energy on other activities, which become distractions in the sense that they distract him from his specific life goal. He does not form a plan, and he does not take steps to bring him closer to reaching his dream. He is, in actuality, sabotaging his own success.

He does not seem aware of the sixth Universal Law, which is this:

The Law Of Focus And Discipline: Keep your eye on the prize. All distractions are equal, and equally counterproductive. Keep yourself under control at all times.

What if Thomas developed enough discipline to spend just half an hour each evening focusing on his dream of becoming a website designer? Not just daydreaming about it, but actively doing something to make that dream come true? He could do a lot in that half hour. For instance, Thomas could:

- *Check out a book at the library that explains the fundamentals of web design (library books are free!)*

- *Do research on the Internet to see what it takes to start a web design business from home*

- *Invite a computer-savvy friend over who knows something about designing websites; treat him to dinner and in exchange ask him to share what he knows about web design*

- *Download free website design software and start tinkering with it*

- *He could take a course with someone already designing websites and not even have to go to college*

There is so much he can do to start moving his life in the direction he'd like to go. Again, his heart is in the right place—he has a desire. But that's not enough. Thomas needs to focus on his dream. He needs to bring discipline into his life so that he's not wasting valuable time he could instead be applying towards his goal.

What Does This Mean For You?

All right, let's say you or your child has a desire for change in your life. You have a specific goal in mind. You envision yourself pursuing and achieving that goal. You affirm yourself with wonderful phrases, such as I can do it! You are definitely on the right track.

Now, take it a step further. As the law states, "Keep your eye on the prize." Don't let it slip away! It's yours for the taking, if you want it. Stay focused on your goal, minimize distractions. In practical terms, this may mean any number of things that you or your child will have to do, such as:

- *Turn off the TV. Limit the time your child plays video games.*

- *Limit the time you and your child surf the Internet— unless its productive surfing that brings you tangible information that will help you reach your goal. I myself was amazed at how much time I save doing this.*

- *Designate a couple of nights a week to call friends; use the other nights to work towards your goal. Or just put a limit on the amount of minutes you or your child spend on the phone.*

- *Limit the number of outside activities your child commits to, so that they do not become over extended.*

- *Get organized—set a specific day for writing letters, paying bills, or catching up on email, then use other days to work towards your goal. Doing something as simple as teaching your young child to lay out the clothes they wish to wear the night before can give you both more time to focus on your goals. I've know many young mothers and children to get distracted trying to find shoes, socks, and even hair ribbons.*

By no means am I advocating that you get rid of all distractions. As each of us well knows, some "distractions" are good for our wellbeing. Prepare yourself a healthy meal. Take a nice, long, relaxing bath. Go out to the movies with a close friend. Take a walk. Read bedtime stories to your children. Watch your favorite weekly television show.

I'm not suggesting that you or your child cut out everything from your life that isn't directly tied to your dream! Well, of course not. You need to be a rounded, balanced individual. You need time with loved ones and time to unwind. What I am saying is that if you look carefully, you can find plenty of time and energy to devote to your goal. It's a matter of instilling in yourself and child the abilities of making priorities, keeping your focus on that goal, and being disciplined enough to pull yourself away from many unnecessary distractions so that you can move ahead and get what you want out of life.

A few words about discipline: In our society, we tend to have a warped view of what discipline means. We may think it means deprivation, sacrifice, or punishment. Teach your child the difference between discipline and punishment. For instance discipline might be practicing their karate kicks for an hour everyday. Punishment might be not getting to watch TV because they did not finish their homework. The truth is, discipline does not have to involve these concepts at all. It can, if you wish, but it does not have to. As a parent I think now would be a good time to search within your own self and ask yourself how you wish to instill the meaning of these two words in your child. Discipline as used in our context means the following:

- *Training, as in training yourself a new system, way of life, or manner of conduct that serves you better*

- *Control, as in having sufficient self-control to focus on a goal in order to reach it*

- *Education, as in educating yourself to other ways of behaving, living, or acting in order to further yourself in some manner*

- *Practice, as in "practice makes perfect"*

- *Willpower, as in having enough willpower to forfeit immediate gratification in favor of long-term success and fulfillment*

- *Self-mastery, as in self-restraint*

When you look at discipline in this way, it puts it in a whole new light, doesn't it? Discipline is not a "bad word" when used effectively and lovingly. The word "disciple" means student, and the word "discipline" means, for our purposes, nurture, educate, foster, teach, and learn. Discipline can be a very good thing, indeed.

Now that you have seen discipline in a new light, you can make it your ally. And teach your child to do the same. When your child or you feel the urge to give up that prize you've been working hard to get, wrap yourself around discipline. Tell yourselves the goal's within reach, and get yourself to work a little more towards it. Offer yourself a small reward at the end—maybe reading a chapter of your favorite book, or enjoying a fruit snack (what's your favorite treat? Keep it handy around your home). There are many ways to stay focused and stay on track. By doing so both you and your child will see that reaching ones goal is worth the effort.

Example: Stella's Dream

More than anything else in life, Stella wanted to be a voice actress. She had a gift, and she'd worked very hard for years to get to where she was. In grade school, junior high, and high school she tried out for every play presented in her community, be it in school, at church, or through various youth programs. Sometimes she got a part, sometimes she didn't, but she kept trying nonetheless.

And she listened. When a teacher or director offered advice, she took it seriously. In this way she improved her acting abilities. In college, she chose to major in theater and once again played a number of roles, from very minor ones to leading characters. She also got involved in the other aspects of theater, from stage building to designing costumes. She loved it. After college, she dove into theater and toured with several troupes. It was a fun, exciting life for her.

But now that she was a mom with young children, Stella didn't want to have to keep touring with traveling theater troupes. She wanted to settle down somewhere. Soon her children would start school, and she wanted to give them a sense of stability and permanence. She didn't want to have to drag them all over the place.

So she decided that voice acting would fit her desired lifestyle perfectly. It was a big plus that she currently lived in "voice-acting central," with a couple of studios not far from her home. She could easily drop her kids off in the morning at daycare (and as they got older, school), head for one of the studios to do some voice acting, then pick up her children and spend the evening together with them.

It was the ideal solution, yet somehow she had a hard time committing to actually doing it. A number of factors kept her from dropping by the studio and inquiring about job openings. One was the lazy, slow days of summer. She was having too much fun enjoying a break, spending long afternoons in the park with her kids, watching Disney movies with them in the evening, and staying up late into the wee hours of the morning reading novels after putting her little ones to bed.

There was nothing wrong with what she was doing. After working hard for years, she needed a break, and this was the perfect time to take it, with her children so young and at home with her. She knew they'd grow up fast, and she made it a priority to spend plenty of quality time with them. The problem was that summer was quickly coming to an end, and she needed to devote some of her time to going out there and securing a job she could start in the fall.

Another factor that was holding her back from visiting the voice recording studio was fear. Even though she had an impressive resume and had played quite a few challenging roles in a number of productions, she had never done voice acting per se. The unknowns scared her. What if they told her they didn't need her, then what would she do?

Finally, she overcame her fears and stopped putting off what she had to do. She asked her best friend if she wouldn't mind coming over one afternoon to watch her children while she visited the studio. In the evenings, after her children went to bed, Stella found several different monologues online and practiced reading each one, using a variety of voices. She also updated her resume and made a few calls to get letters of recommendation.

Once she had everything in place, her friend came by to watch the kids and, armed with credentials and practice, Stella headed over to the voice studio. The timing was great—the studio was about to start casting for a commercial. They gave her an audition, and she got the role.

While there, she discovered that they didn't have enough voice acting parts for her to work at it full-time yet, but they were looking for some extra office help. She applied and got the job. They were flexible on the start date; it was mid-August, and they were fine with her starting in September. This gave her more days to enjoy with her children before having to go back to work fulltime, and it gave her the chance to find just the right daycare for them. When September rolled around, she was ready and eager to begin.

Being at the studio every day, she was the first to know when new parts were available, and thus had first dibs on the parts she wanted and qualified for. By finally overcoming her fears and her sluggishness, she was able to get herself to the studio (with a sharp resume, excellent letters of recommendation, and even some voice-acting practice) and make a positive impression. Her discipline paid off.

The Law At Work In Your Life

In some ways, this is the most common-sense Law we've covered so far. How are you or your child going to get to your desired goals if you don't focus on it? You have to commit to it, and commitment requires a good measure of discipline on your parts.

What we focus on becomes our reality. You can have two people living in the same house, and each one sees the world completely differently. One can see it as a frightening, bad place where people are out to get you and danger lurks at every corner. Meanwhile, the other sees the world as an exciting place full of possibilities and opportunities, and plenty of wonderful people to meet. It all depends on the focus. Your focus does become your reality, in time. As a parent think about your children and find creative ways you can help them learn to focus.

Take a second look at the Universal Law covered in this chapter:

Keep your eye on the prize. All distractions are equal, and equally counterproductive. Keep yourself under control at all times.

When you keep your eye on the prize, you stay on track. Sure, there will be setbacks. You might have to drop everything and tend to a loved one who's been injured or fallen sick. You might have to take a second job to pay for unexpected expenses. You might have to get on your roof and fix the leak that appeared after the last hail storm. Things will happen. BUT, they don't have to derail you permanently. Take care of them, and then get back on track.

Any person who has gotten anywhere in life has had to also deal with setbacks and overcome obstacles. It is the way of life. It is the way people reach their dreams. In the end, these challenges make us stronger. Build your resolve and keep your eye on the prize so that you can continue moving forward through the storms. Baby steps will get you there. Why not teach your child and yourself to look at obstacles, simply as an educational process. A lesson in life, it gives you the gift to think about an issue and solve it, while on your way to attaining your goal.

Practice the Law of Focus and Discipline with your child by following these steps:

1 Pick something that your child and you have wanted to complete for a long time. (Make this an easy one at first for both of you. Especially one that is more attainable for a young child so they do not get frustrated). Perhaps you've wanted to put together a photo album with pictures from your most recent trip. Perhaps you've wanted to re-organize your closet. Or maybe your child and you wanted to familiarize yourselves with some of the constellations that appear in your night sky. Think about

what you've wanted to do together for a while and pick one that currently interests you both the most.

2 Take what you've selected in Step 1, and make the time for it. Schedule it in and make it a priority. Gather the supplies you and your child need to work on your project. If you need more than one session to complete it, then just schedule it in.

3 Continue with your project or learning venture with your child until you've accomplished what you set out to do together... Block out distractions as much as possible. Focus on the task at hand and you'll get it done. Doing it together will make it fun for both parent and child.

4 Write down a list of words with your child, perhaps ten words. Go back and rewrite these same words, only write each word backwards. This is a great exercise for practicing how to focus. For a young child two or three words will be sufficient.

5 Come up with a long-term goal. Your child and you can work on your goals separate here if you like. This may take some time to think of. It must be something you're interested in doing, something you get excited by, something that you truly wish to complete. Once you've chosen your goal, or goals, develop a game plan with your child for reaching it.

6 Take the first step towards your long-term goal, as specified in your game plan. When you've completed that step, cross it off. Then take the next step. Cross it off when it's done. Continue forward with your plan, one step at a time, until you've reached your goal.

Give yourself and your child plenty of time to complete Steps 5 and 6. It may take you a year, or even longer, to get it done. Don't worry about how long it takes you. Simply focus on getting from one point to the next, one step at a time. Focus on the process. The Law of Focus and Discipline is not about overnight success. It is about following a process that will lead you to success. Take the time to practice this Law, giving it the time and attention it deserves.

Affirmations To Use

As you practice becoming more focused and disciplined, the following affirmations can support your child and you in your endeavors. Repeat them as often as you need to until they are part of your psyche. In this way it will help you both to integrate the Universal Law of Focus and discipline into your daily lives. You are both now taking one of the important steps towards fostering the discipline needed and maintaining the focus required to reach your most excellent goals. As always please feel free to make up your own affirmations with your child.

Affirmation 1: I give myself permission to pursue my fabulous goal. My goal matters and I can reach it.

Affirmation 2: At all times, I keep my eye on the prize, knowing I will reach it.

Affirmation 3: I am a winner. I will act like a winner. I will do what I need to do to win the game of life.

Affirmation 4: My mind is finely tuned and focused. I know what I want. I know what I need to do to get it. I have a plan in place. I set it in motion. I take action to reach the prize.

Childs Affirmation: I will reach my goal.

Feel free to let both you and your child's imagination work for you as you affirm your worth and your ability to focus on the prize. Picture yourself as a marathon racer, a champion skater, a long-distance swimmer. Envision yourself with the same level of focus, discipline, and dedication that such athletes develop to reach their goals. You are a winner—treat yourself like one. Act like a winner. Be a winner. Because both of you are winners.

Exercises To Try With Your Child

Like most things in life, focus and discipline take practice. The more you and your child practice these, the better you'll get, and the easier it becomes. Ease into it, and do a little more each day. Before you know it, you've created a new routine for yourself.

Try the following with your child to get up, get motivated, get going, and get some valuable practice in on the Law of Focus and Discipline:

1 **Practice Puzzles.** It doesn't matter what kind of puzzle it is. It could be a crossword puzzle, or Sudoku, maybe Kakuro if you're up to the challenge. A jigsaw puzzle works, too. . Or Rubik's Cube, which enjoyed so much fame and attention years ago. (Now they even have something called Rubik's Sudoku, if you can believe it! It's a board game, actually.)

The point is to find a puzzle and stick with it until you've completed it. Take breaks as needed, but get back to it until you've solved or finished the puzzle. In this way, you'll be training yourself in the art of focus and discipline. A very young child may use a wooden puzzle that has animal shapes.

2 **Try Juggling.** Talk about needing to focus! Juggling is a fantastic way to practice your focus and concentration. If you've never juggled before, start with one ball and move up to two. Two may be enough. Or if you get good at this, move up to three. You could use small stuffed toys to practice learning how to juggle with your child. No one can get hurt that way.

If you already know how to juggle, try new challenges. Move up to juggling four or five balls at a time. Or juggle objects of different sizes. Try a lime, a grapefruit, and a melon—how's that for a challenge that requires intense focus? If you miss, be ready to roll up your sleeves and do a little bit of cleaning. Or why not just place a drop cloth on the floor and have fun with your child. Then you can just fold up the cloth and dispose of any messes. Your child will appreciate you making a game out of this exercise. The bonus is you both will get a lot of laughs out of doing this together.

3 **Learn A New Language.** You don't need to be proficient, just master the basics, like greetings, numbers, colors, things like that. Language software programs are available for purchase, but you'll probably find language tapes at your nearby library which you can borrow for free. Take the time to learn how to say basic phrases with your child by repeating them back and forth with your child, focusing on correct pronunciation. You can practice doing this with your child anywhere. If you want to do something different with this exercise you and your child could learn sign language like one little girl did with her mom when they did this exercise.

Learning another language requires that you immerse yourself completely. You have to train your ear to pick up new sounds. You need to train your tongue to make new sounds that might be a bit challenging, sounds that you don't have in your native language. Have fun, practice this with your child in front of a mirror. Be prepared to see your child make all kinds of funny faces while doing this. Learning the basics of another language is a fantastic way to practice focus and discipline—and to broaden your mind.

Summing It Up

To reach your prize, teach yourself and child to stay focused on your goal and minimize distractions.

If you look carefully, you and your child can find plenty of time and energy to devote to your goal.

It's about making priorities, keeping your focus on that goal, and being disciplined enough to pull yourself away from many unnecessary distractions so that you can move ahead and get what you want out of life.

When you or your child feel the temptation to give up that prize you've been working hard to get, wrap yourself around discipline.

Tell yourself and your child that the goals are within reach, you just need to work a little more towards it.

When you and your child keep your eye on the prize, you stay on track, even when there are setbacks.

Any person who has gotten anywhere in life has had to also deal with setbacks and overcome obstacles. These are only educational gifts in the end, these challenges make us stronger.

Build your resolve and keep your eye on the prize so that you can continue moving forward through the storms.

Both you and your child need to focus on getting from one point to the next, one step at a time. Focus on the process.

Chapter Seven

The Law Of
Taking Action

"Success seems to be connected with action.
Successful people keep moving. They make mistakes, but they don't quit."
— Conrad Hilton

Chapter 7

S alma Hayek had a childhood ambition: to become an actress. Along the way, she went a different direction for a while, studying international relations at a university in Mexico City. This, however, did not interest her enough. She still desired to be an actress. She visualized herself in this role, and she was prepared to focus on what she had to do to reach her ambition.

Even though her parents weren't happy about her decision, she dropped out of college to pursue her acting in earnest. By the time she was 23, she had a major part in a soap opera, making her a household name in Mexico. Having reached her dream at such a young age, she decided to keep going with it and take on new challenges.

She took action by moving to Los Angeles to try to get into Hollywood movies. Salma spent months learning English and perfecting her acting skills. She went from being a well-known star in her native Mexico to a virtual unknown in the United States. Back at square one, she worked her way up through several smaller roles until she got more substantial parts. By being focused on her goal and disciplined in her approach, she once again succeeded, becoming a well-known actress with countless in the U.S. admiring her work.

With both a Golden Globe and an Oscar nomination, and other honors including Glamour Magazine Woman of the Year (2001) and Harvard Foundation Artist of the Year (2006), she certainly could consider herself successful enough to be done and enjoy an early retirement. Instead, she keeps going. When she's not acting, Salma is busy producing movies and television shows. She's won acclaim for her acting and producing talents in the film Frida, as well as the television series Ugly Betty. She has started her own production company, called Ventanarosa. At the rate she's going, the sky's the limit!

Salma Hayek illustrates beautifully the seventh Universal Law:

The Law of Taking Action: Learn to be the most effective in doing what must be done. Once you've made a decision, follow through with action.

Salma has accomplished much in a short time, overcoming language barriers and the challenges that come from starting over in another country. Part of her success can be attributed to her talent, her determination, and the hard work she puts into every acting role and every project she works on. But an equally important factor that contributes to her phenomenal achievements is her willingness to dive in, to leap when necessary, to take action.

Often this is what sets leaders and achievers apart. It is good to plan, analyze, evaluate, and weigh options. Unfortunately, some people never leave this stage. At some point, you have to take action. You must take that leap of faith in order to see what happens next.

What Does This Mean For You?

At any given moment in your life, your child or you are faced with numerous choices. Some are clear choices, others aren't. Which direction do you go? How do you know if it's the right choice? What if it's the wrong decision? One of the ways I make decisions when my head and heart are fighting is to just back off and look at the facts of the decision I am making. Then I ask myself if my child was making this decision and it was their life, not mine, what would I tell THEM to do from a Mother's heart? Then I move forward and do it. Hey, we would never ill advise our children now would we?

It is very important to ask ourselves these questions. But there comes a point when a decision needs to be made and action must be taken. Otherwise, we never leave square one! When we do take action, we get results, and we can better gauge whether or not the decision was sound. We can then ask ourselves:

- *Was this the right choice?*

- *If not, what are my options now?*

- *Have I considered all possible alternatives?*

- *If it is the right choice, then what is my next step?*

- *Where do I go from here?*

Taking action not only advances us forward, it also gives us tangible results we can evaluate. And if some mistakes are made along the way, that is part of the learning experience. Learning from our failures leads us to eventual success. When you teach your child to look at it that way, then there is NO FAILURE, just learning experiences.

The seventh Law speaks in particular of what is most effective. It is in your best interest to act effectively, as this creates more focused energy, which gives you the momentum to move forward more quickly. It also creates the shortest path from where you currently are to where you want to end up.

What defines effective action differs from one person to the next, from one scenario to another. Believe it or not, there are times when it's best to wait. But waiting need not be passive. While you wait for the opportune moment, you can be preparing a plan of action. When the moment presents itself, you are ready to leap!

Other times it is necessary to take action before you're fully comfortable with the idea. If you don't act quickly enough, the opportunity may disappear, or you may change your mind.

115

Either way, you might miss a fantastic opportunity that may not present itself again for a while.

For these reasons, you must trust your intuition. And teach your child to do the same. Ask yourself:

- *What is the best course of action in this particular instance?*

- *Is it best to act now, or to wait?*

- *Do I need to evaluate and modify my plan of action?*

- *What do I need before putting my plan into action?*

- *What do I hope to gain by taking action now?*

- *What are my options?*

- *What do I need to have in place in order for the action I'll take to be most effective?*

Ask yourself these and other questions. Then listen to your intuition. What is it telling you? With practice, you'll learn to trust your intuition. You will know whether you should take immediate action, or whether you should wait. You will also know what it is that you should wait for. And, you'll probably know when you've waited long enough. All of these are personal choices that you must make. You determine your course of action and the right timing. Teaching your child to go inside themselves in this way, will help them make the choice that is right for them.

Don't be afraid to take that first step. The next step is, if something's not working, take a step back. Every so often evaluate where you are. Could there be better options? Is it time to try another direction? When you're clear about where you want to go, the steps to get you there become more clear. Add all of these individual steps together, and you have your plan of action.

Looking at Salma Hayek's real-life example one more time, you'll notice that for her, taking action sometimes involved making tough choices and taking risks. Salma chose to leave college to focus on acting. Many thought this was a huge mistake—but she knew that if she didn't give acting a try, she'd never know if she could make it as an actor. Once Salma had achieved success in Mexican television shows, she wanted to try Hollywood. Again, another tough choice, with a lot of risk involved. In any case, she kept taking action, always keeping her eye on the prize, always learning every step of the way. This process worked for her, and it can work for you.

Example: Doing What He Loves

When he was in high school, Sam had been quite athletic. He was a track star, in fact, doing his best in long-distance running. He did a little running after graduation, but not as much as he would have liked. Sam jumped into training to become an emergency medical technician. Soon he had completed his training, received his license, and was busy working long hours as a paramedic in one of the largest cities in the nation.

He loved his work and moved up quickly. Others were impressed by his quick thinking and quick action. As soon as he got to an accident scene, he was in constant motion, doing everything in his power to help the victims. He won award after award for going above and beyond the call of duty.

His work consumed him, and at first he wanted it that way. But after a while, he felt that something was missing from his life. The long shifts and adrenaline-rushing nature of his work were starting to wear him down. Sam realized he needed a break ... but what?

When he wasn't working, he kept himself occupied with social activities. He played poker with the guys. He went out to the movies, or to grab a bite to eat. He attended baseball games and other sporting events. And, he put on weight.

He weighed 35 pounds more than he did when he graduated from high school. Sam wasn't interested in being a tall, lanky, skinny kid again, but he did want to be closer to his ideal weight, which meant that he needed to lose about 15 pounds. But how could he find the time to do it? He already worked long hours. After hours, he wanted to have fun, clear his mind from the pain and suffering at the accident scenes.

An idea came to him. Why not start running again? He entertained the thought for a moment, but then he felt it was out of reach. He was too old, out of shape, and too busy. His track star days were over. Then he began to notice runners in his neighborhood. When he was driving his ambulance—when he wasn't rushing to emergencies and had a moment to look around—he noticed other people running as well. Young people, old people, incredibly fit people, and overweight people, too. If they can run, he asked himself, why not me?

The next week, he decided to give it a try. He felt a little silly in his shorts, and a little self-conscious about what he was doing. He hadn't run in years. Were the neighbors watching? What would they think? What about his poker team, what would they say if they saw him running?

He put his doubts aside and just started running. And as he ran, all of the excitement and exhilaration he'd once known as a runner came rushing back. It was quite a heady experience for him. He hadn't felt this alive in a long time.

Sam decided to run the next day, and the next. Each day, he ran a little bit longer. Sometimes he had to make a tough choice—hang out with the guys, or go running? Most of the time, he chose to run. After a while, one of his friends decided to join him, Then another. Soon there was a small team of them hooked on running. He never had to run alone, unless he wanted to. With all the exercise he was doing, losing weight became a cinch. But best of all, Sam had re-discovered his passion. He found what was missing from his life, and it was all because he had decided to take action in his life.

The Law At Work In Your Life

You and your child can dream about your goals and life's ambitions all you want. You can prepare yourself well by doing all the necessary internal work. This work is good for you to do. But there comes a time when you have to say, "Now I'm ready." You have to stand up and take action. Without you taking action, your dreams remain just that—pretty dreams. You have to take action in order to move your dreams and goals from the realm of desiring it to the realm of making it happen.

And when you take action, you'll want to do it effectively. It's OK, though, if at first you struggle to find the right path. This is normal. In the right time, you will find the right path. But again, if you don't get your feet wet, if you don't jump in, you won't put things into motion.

Take the time to ask your child one thing they would like to take action on, and then help them get started. Maybe they would like to learn how to play an instrument, or lose weight. They might even want to learn how to garden or become an artist. The choice is theirs.

Another look at the Law of Taking Action:

Learn to be the most effective in doing what must be done. Once you've made a decision, follow through with action.

There it is—follow through with action. You must act. Once you take action, you can continue to evaluate. You can search for the shortest or most effective or best way to get there. Until you do take action, though, you may not get the full picture, or the right perspective.

Until we actually jump in, we don't fully know what's involved. We may have an idea beforehand, but it's difficult to come up with every single possible scenario in our minds. To really know what's going to happen, we have to get the ball rolling. Of course the mental preparation beforehand is important because it does ready us for handling whatever may come.

Here's some ways to help yourself and your child get to know the Law of Taking Action better through doing the following:

1 Do you have some free time coming up—an afternoon, a day, or a weekend? Plan out your chunk of free time such that it requires you to make decisions and take action.

2 For example, say you plan a camping trip. (This is only an example. You pick what you want to do.) It might be fun to ask your child what trip they might like to go on. Ask them what they feel will be needed to do before leaving for your trip? Write out a "to do" list. You might need to:

- Stop by the grocery store or general store to pick up supplies

- Pack, double-checking that you've brought everything

- Bring spares—spare clothes in case it rains, spare shoes, spare tire

- Check your route carefully on the map

- What else?

3 After completing the preparations you listed in Step 2, plan activities to do once you get there. Sticking with our camping example, you might decide to:

- Go fishing

- Go hiking

- Build a campfire

- Search for plants you've not seen before

- Watch wildlife

- Meet people at the campground

- Read a book

- Write in a journal

- Go swimming

- Rent a boat

- What else?

4 When you return home from your trip or your activity, spend some time reflecting on it.

5 Answer these questions: How did your plans go? Did your expectations meet the reality of the experience? What unexpected things came up that you had to deal with? Did you have a chance to do everything you had planned? What did you enjoy most?

6 Once again, think about all of the actions that you took during your free time. Which was most rewarding to you? What was most effective? What would you do differently next time? What would you do the same?

By taking action, we get the chance to experience reality. First we make preparations, then we act, and then we reflect and analyze. In this manner, we discover what we enjoy, and we can make better decisions the next time we act. We can also evaluate what was worthwhile or effective, and what wasn't.

Affirmations To Use

Teach yourself and your child not to be afraid to take action. It's good to first analyze, check your options, weigh your choices, compare one possibility against another, minimize risk, and tune into your intuition. You are wise to do these things. But remember that until you actually take action, nothing will get done. So don't be afraid. There is no need to procrastinate. The following affirmations can help you take that leap of faith and get the ball rolling.

Affirmation 1: I set events into motion in order to create wonderful new possibilities for my life.

Affirmation 2: By taking action, I give myself the gift of a full and fulfilling life

Affirmation 3: Taking action is exciting and fun. It enables me to see the results of my work and savor the fruits of my labor

Childs Affirmation 4: I take action to see what I can do.

Here's another reason to take action—you and your child will both feel a sense of accomplishment, and a sense of relief. You will feel an accomplishment because you're now doing something, and relief because you've actually started the process going. Dreaming is fun, but over-dreaming and over-analyzing can become a burden. When you start to feel this burden or this weight upon your shoulders, that's a clue that it's time to take action. Every thing starts with taking that first step.

Exercises To Try With Your Child

There are no shortcuts to taking action. To make this Universal Law work, you have to get up and take action. It's as simple as that. So the next exercises strive to do just that—get you into the habit of taking action.

1 **Volunteer.** In any community, there are more volunteer opportunities available than volunteers to fill them. Think about a volunteer job you would like to get involved in. Building houses with Habitat for Humanity? Serving meals to homeless people at a community kitchen? Growing vegetables in a community garden? Helping out at the humane society?

Pick a volunteer opportunity of your choice or better yet why not let your child pick one? And sign up for it. Get involved, and make a difference.

2 **Take Up A Sport.** It doesn't have to be a competitive sport, unless you want it to be. Recreational is just fine. The point is to take something up where you and your child can have fun, get some exercise, and maybe even meet people. There are many sports and fitness activities to choose from—tennis, golf, speed walking, weight lifting, swimming, recreational team sports such as basketball, soccer, or volleyball. Pick one, and go for it.

3 **Write A Letter.** Can you think of a good way to resolve a thorny issue in your community? Share your ideas with others through a letter to the editor. Want to thank someone for a kind act or a special favor? Write them a really nice thank you note. It'll make you feel good, and it'll make their day. Haven't heard from a relative in a while? Write that person a cheerful letter. Why not write your child a thank you note thanking them for the things they do for you? With so many people, sending computer

e-mails, text messages and even faxes to say thank you, it's good to teach your child how much more personal it is to send a hand written one. You and your child should write a letter to each other each month to say thanks for being in my life. Then state in the letter all the qualities you admire in each other and what you did for each other that month that made your heart smile.

Summing It Up

Often what sets leaders and achievers apart is their willingness to take action.

At some point, you have to take action. You must take that leap of faith in order to see what happens next.

When we do take action, we get results, and we can better gauge whether or not the decision was sound.

If mistakes are made along the way, that is part of the learning experience. Learning from our failures leads us to eventual success.

Acting effectively creates more focused energy, which gives you the momentum to move forward more quickly.

It also creates the shortest path from where you currently are to where you want to end up.

Don't be afraid to take that first step, and the next step, and the one that comes after that.

You have to take action in order to move your dreams and goals from the realm of desiring it to the realm of making it happen.

Once you take action, you can continue to evaluate your progress. You can search for the shortest or most effective or best way to get there.

Chapter Eight

The Law Of Worthiness

"Self-worth comes from one thing —
thinking that you are worthy."
—Wayne Dyer

Nikola Tesla was a brilliant scientist and inventor who harnessed the power of electricity and magnetism to transform the world. His epiphanies led to the development of the induction motor, a key component today in everything from power tools to washing machines to electric cars. He researched and championed the use of alternating current for the generation of electricity. A true genius, Nikola aptly set the foundation for the modern electrical conveniences we enjoy today.

Often dubbed America's "greatest electrical engineer," this Serb born in Croatia in 1856 had dozens of patents to his name. A deep thinker, he developed many principles and devices that advanced the use of electricity and made the development of radio technology possible. Despite his amazing intellect and his outstanding contributions to science and technology, he had his idiosyncrasies. For one, he refused to accept the Nobel Peace Prize when it was offered to him, foregoing the prestige and funds the award would have brought him.

Why is it that we often refuse the very gifts that are presented to us? Nikola had his reasons. What about you—what reasons do you have for refusing to accept gifts the universe bestows upon you?

All right, maybe you haven't been offered the Nobel Peace Prize—yet—but perhaps someone offered you help that you declined. Maybe somebody was willing to cook you a meal when you were sick, or mow your lawn while you recovered from an injury, or even pick up a few items for you at the grocery store. Did you take them up on their offer?

Let's broaden the picture a bit. Perhaps you were offered a scholarship, a job position, or a recognition award, but you declined, not because you didn't want it, but because you felt you didn't deserve it. Or maybe you won a contest of some sort, but you never picked up the prize. Why?

Again, you may have your reasons, and they may be valid. But many people around the world refuse wonderful gifts; including love, praise, thanks, and yes, material possessions also, for one basic reason: they feel unworthy. By the way did you ever think by not excepting something from someone you could be being selfish? I bet not. But let us look at it a different way for a moment. When you do something for someone or give them something how do you feel? Good, right? So when someone want to do something for you or give you something it's selfish not to accept it because by not doing so you do not allow them to feel good. That puts a different outlook on things now doesn't it?

The eighth Universal Law addresses this phenomenon:

The Law Of Worthiness: You must be worthy to receive all the gifts the universe has for you. Abundance is a reality, and you must be open to receive.

When one doesn't feel worthy enough, or valuable or important enough, to receive good things that are out there, we miss the rewards we've worked so hard to enjoy. Had Nikola accepted his award, he would have received funds to support the experiments he so took pleasure in conducting. At least for a time he would have been released from having to scrape and scrounge to support his independent research, and instead would have enjoyed the luxury of dedicating himself fully to his scientific investigations. Being a Nobel Peace Prize recipient—even if he did have to split the honor and prize money with his friend turned nemesis, Thomas Edison—would have given him the clout he needed for financiers to come forward and fund his many experiments. But for whatever reason, he was unable to accept the prize and as a result he had to work much harder to advance in his inspired work.

Now let's look at Bill Gates, His growing commitment to world causes is evident in his decision to step down from the day-to-day operations of Microsoft in order to devote more of his time and energy to the Foundation starting in 2008. After years of building his business empire, Bill has found a new calling in life. As a socially responsible philanthropist, he's turned to the business of giving hope and dignity to the people of the world.

Bill's "conversion" brings us to discuss the ninth Universal Law:

The Law Of Giving And Receiving: What you give, you also receive back in kind. Energy flows in the universe, with giving and receiving perpetually recycling in this constant flow.

Bill Gates is, financially, the richest man in the world. But what good is wealth if he was unable to accept the prize, and as a result, he had to work much, much harder to advance his important work.

Here are some of the reasons we may refuse a gift the universe presents to us:

- *A misguided sense of humility*
- *Pride, arrogance*
- *Anger, bitterness*
- *Fear, mistrust*
- *Not ready for it*
- *Comes with too much responsibility*
- *Will force us to change*

These entire different reasons boil down to one primary cause: lack of trust. Either we do not trust ourselves enough, or we do not trust the universe enough. In each case, the inability to trust emanates from a mentality of "lack," and this comes from a position of "unworthiness."

Let's flip the coin over. What if you felt worthy enough to receive all that life, the universe, and everything has to offer you? What if you weren't too humble to accept a gift? What if pride, arrogance, fear and mistrust did not obstruct your viewpoint? What if you felt completely ready for it? What if you welcomed the responsibility that came with the gift? What if you also welcomed the changes the gift would inevitably bring into your life?

I would say that you would be more than ready to grow and progress! Those who can accept the gifts that come their way are the people who know how to seize opportunities and get where they're going. Ultimately, they become the success stories.

But did you know that it might even be selfish not to accept a gift from someone?

Let me share with you how I found out that not accepting a gift, even the gift of help from someone, was a selfish thing.

When my daughter Jennifer died all of my friends wanted to help me by cooking food, taking care of my pets, one friend even offered to do my laundry. I always said no thanks to my friends when they asked to do something for me. Then one good friend of mine told me I was being selfish as I was not letting anyone help me.

What Does This Mean For You?

Whether you feel "worthy" or "unworthy" may well stem back to your childhood. How did your parents or teachers respond to you when you hoped for approval? Did they give it to you willingly, or did they deny it from you? Did they applaud your

130

achievements, conduct, curiosity, and effort, or did they respond in a way that made you feel you didn't deserve their approval?

These and other childhood experiences have a way of storing themselves deep into our psyche. We may forget the actual events, but subconsciously we are trained to "expect" either success or failure, either reward or disappointment. If you've lived a pattern of feeling unworthy, know that this pattern probably goes back—way back—to a point you no longer can trace. But even though the pattern may be ingrained in you deeply, you CAN make changes, starting today. Knowing all this also allows you as a parent to learn how not to do this to your own child. See how great learning these Universal Laws together can be? If you have not already instilled these feelings in your child because of a lack of proper upbringing yourself, now you will get the chance to change it in your child before they repeat the pattern with their own children.

Begin with this simple but very powerful exercise. Close your eyes and picture something you want: A genuine smile from a stranger, perhaps. A compliment on your work performance from your boss, a beautiful red rose. An item you've wanted to purchase but felt was too much of a luxury. Now, picture yourself receiving the gift, be it the compliment, the rose, whatever it is you want. And as you receive this gift in your mind, repeat to yourself out loud: I am worthy. I AM worthy to receive this bountiful gift!

Truly, you are deserving of the many wonderful gifts the universe has to offer you. If you think that you are not, then you must reprogram your thinking and your response to your feelings. For all of the other Universal Laws covered in this book to work for you, it is very important that you feel you deserve to receive good things. Otherwise, you create a block and the universe cannot get past this self-imposed blockage. It will wait patiently for you, but it will not break through the barriers you've set up.

In order to receive, you must be willing to receive. You must consider yourself worthy of the gifts presented to you. This is neither arrogance nor selfishness. This is more akin to gratitude, which we'll cover in depth in a future chapter. Be grateful for the gifts presented to you, and be gracious in accepting them. You, like every one of your spiritual brothers and sisters, are worthy of receiving good things in your life. Be open to them. Be receptive.

Example: Harder To Receive

Kristin was always thinking of others. Every birthday, every time a baby was born, every graduation, wedding anniversary, job well done, you name it, she would send off a little something, booties for the new baby, a touching poem for the graduate, a card with money in it. She was a big-hearted person, a fantastic giver. But when it came to receiving, it was another story. She didn't know how to receive graciously.

When neighbors brought her bags of oranges from their backyard trees, she felt she had to make something—orange pound cake, or orange marmalade, for example—and share it with them to return the favor. If someone took care of her plants while she was gone, Kristin showed up at their door with a lavish, expensive gift wrapped in fancy paper and adorned with a huge bow. Funny thing was, if someone had brought her a gift like that, she wouldn't know how to accept it.

What's more, she had a really tough time saying the words "thank you." Kristin would get all flustered. She'd get very talkative, moving the conversation on to another topic (How's your Aunt Flora doing after her knee operation?) just to get away from having to thank the other person for the gift.

Kristin didn't realize it, but her reluctance to receive went back to her childhood days. Her mother had been a good but stern woman. She'd been very strict with her children, just as her mother had been with her. She taught them to be happy with little—not a bad thing necessarily, except that "little" is what Kristin came to expect out of life. She did not feel deserving of the good things that came her way. She felt she hadn't "earned" them. This put her at a disadvantage time and time again.

Finally, in her later years, she began to realize what she'd been doing her entire life. And she began to give herself permission to live a little, to receive with no strings attached. The more she opened herself up to receiving, the easier it got to accept presents. She even learned how to say "thank you" and leave it at that. Kristin learned that in this world, there is a time to give, and a time to receive graciously.

The Law At Work In Your Life

Many people live with a consciousness of lack. They say to themselves, and to whoever is willing to listen, statements such as these:

I wish I had more money. If I just had more money, I'd …

I don't get enough love from my spouse. I don't get appreciated. If I could find a better partner in life, I could …

I never have enough time. People are always bugging me to do more. If I had more free time, I would …

And so on, and so forth. Why live this way? Why blame others for one's own lack of self-worth? Why focus on lack, when the universe is willing and ready to give us so much, if only we let it?

If you find yourself or your child acting with a mentality of lack, it's time to change. You have been missing out on a lot of "free gifts." Stop depriving yourself. See the universe for what it truly is—a richly bountiful place. Think about it. Every spring, new plants pop up from the ground. Every summer, we are blessed with warmth and sunshine. Every fall, corn and apples and pumpkins are harvested. Every winter, people head to the mountains to play in the snow. Every season offers up plentiful delights. Abundance is the way of the Earth. Welcome it, and receive it.

Look at the Law of Worthiness once again:

You must be worthy to receive all the gifts the universe has for you. Abundance is a reality, and you must be open to receive.

Do you see how you are the gatekeeper? When you open the doors wide, you allow abundance to enter into your life. You hold the key. If you keep the doors locked shut, then you can't expect good things to come your way, can you?

Now turn it around. When you do keep those doors open, then you have every right to expect good things, right? Keep the door open, my friend. Let the universe present you with all of the abundance you so deserve.

1   Doing these next steps with your child, will help put you and your child more at ease with the Law of Worthiness:

2   Picture in your mind's eye something you'd like to have in your life right now. Focus on it with all your might. Make it as real as possible. What would your life be like if this was in your life? In what way would it serve you?

3   Next, give yourself permission to have this in your life. Ask yourself formally, "May I have this." Answer yourself directly, "Yes, you may have this. It is yours."

4   Now that you've given yourself permission, devise a plan and take action. What do you need to do to bring this into

your life? Once you've developed a plan, set it into motion. What's your first step? Your second? The one after that?

5 If the initial plan is not working out as you'd hoped, revise it. Make it more effective. Then, take action again. Work towards getting that which you wish to have.

6 Take a moment to check your status: Are you still receptive? Remind yourself that you are worthy to receive.

7 Once you have attained that which you wished for, give thanks. Be grateful for what the universe has given you.

You and your child can apply these six steps over and over again for many different things in your life. Perhaps you wish for a promotion, or greater responsibility at work. Perhaps you wish to get a new couch. Maybe you want a puppy. First visualize it, then tell yourself you are worthy, and then devise a plan. Once you put your plan into motion, continue to tell yourself that you are worthy of receiving what you desire.

Affirmations To Use

The time is NOW for you to tell yourself that you are worthy of receiving the good gifts which the universe presents before you. As you tell yourself the following affirmations, internalize them. Trust them. Believe them with everything you have.

Have faith in yourself, teach your child to have faith in themselves, and have faith in the reality around you. For as your good thoughts go out, so they return to you in like. And as your words of encouragement and empowerment enter your soul, you will find the strength to accept the riches which life has to offer.

Affirmation 1: I am open to the goodness of the universe. I accept the riches that come my way. I accept and appreciate each gift I receive.

Affirmation 2: The basic fabric of the universe is love. The basic nature of the universe is abundance. The basic tenet of life is joy. I accept it.

Affirmation 3: I am worthy of all the gifts the universe brings my way.

Affirmation 4: I accept the gifts others bring to me with an open heart.

Childs Affirmation: I am happy for all the gifts I receive.

Remember, if you are uncomfortable with receiving gifts, think of it this way. How do you feel when you present somebody with a gift? You probably feel good inside, right? It stands to reason, then, that the person giving you a present feels good inside because of the act of giving. If you cannot accept this gift openly, then you are denying the other person the pleasure of giving. Each of us has to learn to receive, as well as to give, in order to better enjoy the interaction between one another. So go on, feel worthy of the gift, for your sake and for the sake of whomever, or whatever, is doing the giving.

Exercises To Try With Your Child

Think of these as esteem-building exercises. You are building yourself up so that you can be receptive to blessings, opportunities, and other gifts. I can't say it enough—you are so deserving of all the good things that are headed your way! Convince yourself of this. Make it a fact. Everyone deserves goodness. Why not you? Try these exercises; they'll convince you even further.

1 **Treat Yourself and Your Child.** What do you enjoy? Do you like good music? Then treat yourself to an evening at the symphony. Do you enjoy plays? Give yourself permission to go watch one. Ask your child to think about something they would really like to do, but which they don't get to do very often (or at all), Then, indulge them and yourself by doing it. You and they deserve it.

2 **Write A Story.** Get creative here—write a story about yourself where you're the star! And then ask your child to do the same. You are the hero or heroine who saves the day. You are the one who comes up with a brilliant solution. You are a talented, charming person adored by many. Go ahead, make up a good one. Enjoy the attention your character, you, receive from your good deeds or brilliant escapades. Then tell each other your story. You and your child can do this on a regular basis, and even make your own book out of the stories you write.

3 **Surprise Yourself and Child Sometimes.** Do something completely on impulse. For example, stop by a coffee shop on your way home and get yourself a delicious cup of coffee or tea. Or stop by a beautiful park before getting home and take a long walk with your child. Have you noticed how your child often surprises you by drawing you a picture or even giving you a hug? Praise them for this and let them know how good it makes you feel.

The main thing is to do something unexpected. Surprise yourself by doing something unplanned, something out of the ordinary routine. It's a gift you give yourself, because you are worthy and so is your child!

Summing It Up

When we don't feel worthy enough, or valuable or important enough, to receive good things that are out there, we miss the rewards we've worked so hard to enjoy.

The inability to trust emanates from a mentality of "lack," and this comes from a position of "unworthiness."

Those who can accept the gifts that come their way are the people who know how to seize opportunities and get where they're going. Ultimately, they become the success stories.

You are deserving of the many wonderful gifts the universe has to offer you.

If you think that you are not, then you must reprogram your thinking and your response to your feelings.

In order to receive, you must be willing to receive. You must consider yourself worthy of the gifts presented to you.

Be grateful for the gifts presented to you, and be gracious in accepting them.

You, like every one of us, are worthy of receiving good things in your life. Be open to them. Be receptive.

See the universe for what it truly is—a richly bountiful place.

Chapter Nine

The Law Of
Giving and Receiving

What you give out you get back ten times over in life

Chapter 9

When we think of a selfless giver, we might think of Mother Teresa, or a Peace Corps volunteer, or a Habitat for Humanity when it's kept to oneself. Certainly he enjoys a comfortable life, lacking nothing in the material sense. He's learned, though, that this isn't enough. When he began to give of himself to causes he believes in, he began to get back wealth of another sort, the kind that touches the heart and soul. He has the satisfaction of knowing that he's addressing world problems that are not being adequately dealt with by other groups. Put simply, he's making a difference in the world, and this is worth more than a mountain of hundred dollar bills in the bank.

How else might we word the Law of Giving and Receiving? Here are several possibilities:

- *Give freely—a smile, a kind word, free professional advice, a back rub to your spouse—and see how abundantly you receive*

- *Give with an open heart and a cheerful outlook, and receive in the same spirit*

- *The energy you release is the same energy that returns to you*

- *Be open to receiving, and you'll have more to give*

- *The more you give, the more you are able to receive*

Because giving and receiving, receiving and giving, involve a flow of energy, the practice keeps the soul alive. There is an interaction, an exchange, that takes place, and invariably it involves someone else. Many people report that when they stop giving, they feel dead inside. The flow has stopped. To start

141

that flow again and feel aliveness within us, all we must do is start to give. It makes little difference whether we give praise, a dollar, or a seven-course gourmet meal we've spent hours preparing—so long as it's given from the heart.

What Does This Mean For You?

Just as water and air are necessary to sustain you physically, giving and receiving are paramount to your spiritual health. The exchange of energy that takes place during an instance of giving and receiving has the power to heal. Have you ever seen a grumpy old man soften immediately when his grandchild gives him a great big hug? Or watch a political candidate turn civil during a debate when a contender offers up genuine praise? The right gift at the right moment can soften the hardest of hearts and diffuse nearly any situation. Every gift, freely given, can bring both the recipient and the giver tremendous benefit.

Likewise, every gift gratefully received also benefits both giver and receiver. It goes back to the healing power of the exchange. Look at a child's birthday party, for example. The birthday kid feels special with all the gifts she's been given. Her friends feel special for choosing gifts that are fun and meaningful. At the next party, some of the roles will change—another child will be the recipient of gifts, and the child who got presents this time will have the opportunity to select a fun, meaningful gift for someone else. Life is this way; we all take turns giving and receiving. It's joyous, it's rewarding, and it's empowering.

There doesn't have to be a long delay from the moment we give to the moment we receive back. The gratification can be instant. It can come back in the form of a smile on a child's face, a nod of thanks from someone at the grocery store, a feeling of fulfillment that comes from knowing you did the right thing. All of these are rewards in and of themselves.

Just as some people are not very good at receiving, some folks aren't too good at giving. They are known as "takers" and they haven't yet mastered the art of this two-way interaction. A person who continuously takes and fails to give can be labeled as greedy, selfish, and short-sighted. Mainly, though, such a person is empty. It doesn't matter how much he or she gets, because all the stuff in the world won't fill him or her up. The only way such a person will ever feel full inside, and feel complete, is to start giving.

Example: Young Thomas

Thomas was an active, curious preschooler. He had a tremendous zest for life and enjoyed any kind of hands-on project, from doing puzzles to working with clay to creating works of art with construction paper, crayons, and stickers. Outside he loved to run, play, ride tricycles, and swing on the monkey bars. He was strong and healthy, and his laugh was infectious.

All of his preschool teachers adored him, but they were concerned by one aspect of his personality: Thomas didn't share very well. He was constantly looking to see what he could get. At snack time, if he wasn't one of the first children to be served, he immediately shot his hand up in the air and yelled, "Me, teacher, me, me! I want a snack!" If another child wanted to play with the puzzle or game he was working on, he glared at the child and stomped away with the toy. Often he pushed other kids, and sometimes he took away what they were playing with.

The teachers worked patiently to correct his behavior. They had faith in their teaching abilities and in Thomas's learning abilities. He was, after all, only three years old. He would learn no doubt about it. But why was it taking him longer than the other children to learn to share? What approach could they take to teach him the joys of sharing, the joy of giving?

The teachers—there were three at this particular preschool—came up with a plan. Why not make Thomas a classroom helper? He always wanted to be in the midst of everything. He had plenty of energy, and he did cooperate well with his teachers, even if he didn't share well with his classmates. Maybe giving him more responsibility was the way to gently teach Thomas that giving was as much fun as receiving.

They tried this approach. Thomas was given extra responsibilities in class. He passed out papers, or safety scissors, or glue. He helped put away toys. Usually the first one in class, he helped his peers hang up coats and jackets when they came in.

Thomas never complained about any of the tasks he had to perform. In fact, he seemed to exude a level of pride at being able to help others. This was very good. The teachers were pleased to see him make progress with the idea of giving.

Then there came the big test. It was a classmate's fourth birthday, and the child's parents brought juice and cupcakes to share with the class. Thomas was asked to distribute napkins while the birthday child passed out treats, with help from her parents. How would Thomas do watching everyone else get a cupcake while he was still passing out napkins? Would it be hard on him to see everyone getting a cupcake while he had to wait for his?

His teachers watched him proudly. Thomas took his job seriously. He patiently passed out napkins, making sure every person In that room even the visiting parents—had a napkin before he sat down to enjoy his cupcake. It didn't matter to him that other children had already started eating. He wanted to make sure that he had finished his job before sitting down to enjoy the celebration. With the assistance and patience of his teachers, Thomas had learned that there is a time to get and a time to give.

The Law At Work In Your Life

They say that everything we need to know we learned in kindergarten (or perhaps preschool or maybe first grade for those who didn't attend preschool or kindergarten). In any case, many of us learned to give and receive in those early school days. We learned to share. At the very least, we were exposed to the lessons. As with all life lessons, some people learn them better than others.

If you have a hard time with either giving or receiving, or both, realize that it might be because of one of several possible reasons. It could be that:

- *You were never taught these lessons well enough*

- *At some point, you may have been forced to give something up that you didn't want to relinquish*

- *Someone you neither liked nor trusted gave you a gift, and you were uncomfortable receiving it*

- *Others seemed to have more than you, so you learned to take in order to have*

- *It seemed people liked you only when you gave them something*

- *A parent, teacher, sibling, or friend taught you that to get ahead in life, you have to take, take, take*

A teacher or parent taught you that it's not polite to take without being offered something, and perhaps even made you feel that the first image that comes to mind when we hear "noble giver" is that of Bill Gates! In fact, some of us would sooner picture ourselves throwing our crashing computers at him than think of him as a selfless philanthropist.

But before you pass judgment, take a look at what the founder of Microsoft Corporation, the world's largest software company, is doing globally through the Bill & Melinda Gates Foundation he and his wife started in the year 2000:

- *Funding efforts to eradicate polio throughout the world*

- *Supporting the Global Alliance for Vaccines & Immunizations*

- *Providing funds for HIV research*

- *Donating a billion dollars for scholarships to high achieving minority students*

- *Funding efforts to develop crops and agricultural technologies that better serve the developing world guilty for taking something out of turn.*

Or the reason could have been completely different. Whatever may have happened or failed to happen in the past that now makes it hard for you to be an equal player in the game of giving and receiving, let it go. If you were taught incorrectly, you can now relearn. If an event triggered your mistrust with the act of giving and the act of receiving, you can now correct that. Those negative emotional lessons taught to you as a child could last a life time if you allow it. Don't beat yourself up over them, just learn now how to change your way of thinking. Let go of the old negative lessons learned as a child and replace them with positive ones. Then as a parent teach your own children how to avoid them all together. Remember no one can ever make you think or feel anything as that choice is ALWAYS yours.

Here's another look at the Law of Giving and Receiving:

What you give, you also receive back in kind. Energy flows in the universe, with giving and receiving perpetually recycling in this constant flow.

146

If you give because you feel obligated to, then don't be surprised when others give to you grudgingly. If you give in anger, spite, or with any kind of malice, then spite, anger, and malice will return to you. If instead you give from the heart with a cheerful disposition, you will receive a gift in kind, given to you in the same spirit of love.

What would you like to receive back in kind? Would you like love? Respect? Attentiveness? Courtesy? Generosity? Cordiality? Then be sure to give in this vein.

Six secret steps to do with your child that will give you both a better understanding of the use of the Law of Giving and Receiving. All you have to do is take the first step:

1 Always say "thank you." When you are presented with a gift, no matter how big or small, make sure you let the giver know that the gift is appreciated. When your child gives you a gift, remember to say thank you.

2 Think of ways to give to others. Children love to give to others. Why not ask them each day what they like to give someone? Spontaneous acts of kindness can make the best presents. Give a compliment. Give a flower. Give a smile. Teach your child to give the gift of their smile to everyone they meet. Give your child the gift of feeding the birds.

3 Picture in your mind the symbol for infinity, which looks like the number 8 on its side, something like this: ∞. Envision yourself standing at the rightmost point of the symbol, and a second person standing opposite you at the leftmost point.

4 Send a gift to this person, and watch the gift traverse the path of the infinity sign until it reaches the recipient. Then watch the person send you a gift in return, which

comes back along the other side of the symbol, making a "full circle." This is an effective way to picture the interconnectedness of the give and take process. Let your child draw this on a sheet of paper, then explain to them how everything they give out comes back to them.

5 Make a list of the many gifts you have received this week. They may include a phone call from a friend, birds singing outside your window, a rose in bloom in a garden you walked past, the first snow of the season, a baby smiling at you, or any other gifts you notice.

6 Make a list of the many gifts you have given this week, including a word of encouragement, a hug to console a child, a moment of your time for a stranger with a question, and so on.

7 Write down why you are grateful for all that you received and all that you gave this week.

By giving from the heart, you set a chain of events into motion that touches an untold number of people. Your gift helps the recipient, who in turn is inspired to give to someone, who then gives to someone else. This goes on and on, and like the path of the infinity sign; it eventually comes back to you. It's good to be in this loop of giving and receiving. Doing these six steps with your child will make your own lives happier, and will set off a loving chain reaction to benefit the world in the process.

Affirmations To Use

For some of you, it may be easier to give. For others, it might feel more natural to receive. But in this life, you must do both, give and receive. It is a give and take, a dance every human being dances at various stages of life, sometimes at the giving end, other times at the receiving end. To be fully whole, you must master both.

The following affirmations will help you, wherever you may be in your progress. Whether you wish to become a more humble giver or a more gracious receiver, saying these affirmations (quietly or out loud) will help you to gain mastery of the ninth Universal Law, the Law of Giving and Receiving.

> **Affirmation 1:** I am an equal participant in the game of life. The rules are simple: give abundantly, and receive graciously.

> **Affirmation 2:** It is a joy to give. It is simple to give. As of this moment, I will give compliments, kind words, smiles, encouragement, support, and positive energy freely. As I give, so shall I receive.

> **Affirmation 3:** It is a joy to receive. It is simple to receive. As of this moment, I will receive compliments, kind words, smiles, encouragement, support, and positive energy gratefully. As I receive, so shall I give to others.

> **Affirmation 4:** Giving and receiving transcend words, languages, cultures, and borders. I give and receive from my heart.

> **Childs Affirmation:** It's a joy to give and receive from my heart.

Practice the act of giving and receiving with your child on a regular basis. It may feel uncomfortable at first. But what happens when you practice anything? You get better at it. You feel more comfortable with it. What you practice becomes second nature. By affirming yourself with the sayings above, and actively practicing giving and receiving, you will bring greater joy into your life and more wholeness into your soul.

Exercises To Try with your child

Giving can be a lot of fun. These exercises are designed to help you and your child to learn how to give freely, with no strings attached. This type of giving is the best there is, hands down! Practice them as often as you wish.

1 **Give To A Neighbor Or Shut-In.** Is there someone who recently moved into your neighborhood and whom you haven't met? Are there people who've lived nearby for years whom you haven't had the chance to meet yet? Is there a shut-in that you know of, a person who doesn't get out much because of age, limitations, or other reasons, who might enjoy a visit and a little gift?

Once you've thought of someone, think of a gift to bring them. Nothing fancy, just something meaningful from the heart. It could be cookies you've baked or a simple meal you've prepared. It could be flowers or vegetables from your garden. Maybe a poem you wrote or a stirring picture you drew. Ask your child to help you with ideas on who to give to and on what to give.

Take your gift to this person. If you're invited inside, visit for a while. The company of another human being may be the greatest gift to give this particular family or individual.

If you're simply greeted at the door, that's fine too. Maybe they're busy or they like privacy. In any case, you've made a wonderful connection just by delivering your gift. Know that you've probably made this person's day, maybe even their entire week.

2 **Give The Gift Of Forgiveness.** We've all been hurt by someone, or several somebodies. The hurt can be minor or major, and it can last for many, many years. Think about someone who has hurt you. Take a step of forgiveness towards that person. If you are able to, forgive completely. If this is too much, don't worry. Don't push it. Just thinking about forgiveness in general terms is an empowering first step. Remember one of the greatest gifts of forgiveness is forgiving you.

When you give the gift of forgiveness, you're not letting the other person off the hook. You are letting yourself off the hook. The wrongdoing no longer holds power over you. You give yourself the gift of freedom.

3 **Give Hugs.** To embrace and to be embraced with unconditional love is like getting a glimpse of the love that exists in heaven. Bring a touch of heaven to Earth—hug someone! Hug your spouse or significant other. Hug your child or grandchild. Hug your parent or grandparent. Hug a friend. Hug a friend in need. Hug your animal friend. Hug a stuffed animal or pillow.

And when you embrace, feel unconditional love present in that hug. What a special moment. What a priceless gift. Practice hugging your child everyday.

4 **GIVE TO NATURE.** Plant trees with your child and feed the birds. Clean up the park.

Summing It Up

When you give from the heart, you get back the kind of wealth that touches the heart and soul.

Because giving and receiving involve a flow of energy, the practice keeps the soul alive.

If you feel dead inside, try giving. This will start the flow of energy going again.

The exchange of energy that takes place during an instance of giving and receiving has the power to heal.

Every gift, freely given, can bring both the recipient and the giver tremendous benefit.

Every gift gratefully received also benefits both giver and receiver.

By giving from the heart, you set a chain of events into motion that touches an untold number of people.

To be fully whole, you must master both giving and receiving.

Chapter Ten

The Law Of Gratitude

"Wake at dawn with a winged heart
And give thanks for another day of loving."
— Kahlil Gibran

Perhaps you've taught your own children prayers of thanks or other prayers you may have learned, depending on your background. This simple prayer, like countless others, has a spirit of gratitude woven in. Prayers of gratitude help us remember to thank God, Allah, Buddha, Yahweh, the Great Spirit, Goddess, Jehovah, the Great I AM, the Creator, the One, the Eternal, for all that we have.

They say attitude is everything; an attitude of gratitude can change your perception for the better. Adopting a mindset and heart set of being grateful can make us more pleasant, calmer people. It can lower blood pressure and foster better health. It can remind us of the vast expanse of the universe and how amazing it is to have each planet, each person, and each flower petal precisely in the right place at the right time. An attitude of gratitude reminds us of our cosmic connection to all there is.

The tenth Universal Law is exactly about this very thing:

The Law Of Gratitude: Always be grateful for the blessings we have each day. Live your life with an attitude of gratitude.

Scientists are researching gratitude and finding interesting results. Two psychologists, Dr. Robert A. Emmons of the University of California at Davis and Dr. Michael E. McCullough of the University of Miami, conducted the Research Project on Gratitude and Thankfulness. This is just some of what their research uncovered:

> • *People who kept "gratitude lists" were more likely to make progress toward personal goals in a two-month period compared to those who didn't keep such lists.*

155

- *People who are grateful report higher levels of positive emotions, life satisfaction, vitality, and optimism. At the same time, they report lower levels of depression and stress.*

- *Those who have a grateful disposition are more likely to say they believe in the interconnectedness of all life, and to feel a commitment to and responsibility to others.*

- *There is a difference between feeling grateful and feeling indebted to someone. Gratefulness leads to higher levels of appreciation, happiness, and love. Feeling indebted leads to higher levels of anger.*

- *People who kept gratitude journals on a weekly basis reported a better sense of wellbeing in their lives. They exercised more, noted fewer physical symptoms, and felt better about their lives than did people who logged neutral or negative events in their journals.*

What Does This Mean For You?

Science is just starting to catch up on what religions, philosophies, and traditions have known for eons: That being genuinely grateful is good for your body, mind, and soul. There is tremendous power in gratitude—power to change, power to heal, power to turn your life around and get the most out of each day. Teaching your child to have an attitude of gratitude will give them the edge to deal with life's little stresses.

The power of gratitude includes the following:

- *A respect for your body and a desire to take better care of yourself*

- *A sense of delight for the people around you*

- *The ability to manage stress in your life and cope with daily problems*

- *An optimistic outlook*

- *A boost to your immune system*

- *Seeing beauty and grace where others may miss it*

When you count your blessings each and every day, you boost yourself up. You create positive energy that in turn gives you energy to do everyday tasks as well as handle unexpected challenges. You elevate the positive chemicals in your body, improving your overall wellness, strengthening your immunity, and elevating your mood. You also deflect negative energies and shield yourself against stress and the diseases it causes.

What are some of the characteristics you might find in a person who displays an attitude of gratitude? Ask your child what characteristics they think someone might have. Then ask them to name three people they think has an attitude of gratitude and why they think they have it.

Here's a list of some characteristics that a person with an attitude of gratitude might have.

- *A peaceful demeanor*

- *A light-hearted attitude*

- *A gentle, patient approach with people*

- *A positive outlook*

- *Resiliency during and after difficult times*

- *A sense of humor*

- *The ability to handle stress better*

- *An appreciation for what they have*

- *An overall sense of satisfaction*

- *An ability to value their relationships*

Ask your child what would they add to this list? We all enjoy being around people who appreciate what they have and exude an aura of peace. We like to bask in the glow of their positive energy. Most of us would like to be more like these individuals. To do so, start with a sense of gratitude.

Be grateful for what you have now as well as for what you've enjoyed in the past, even the relationships, friends, jobs, and possessions you no longer have. They served you well, and they had a place in your life. They helped you grow into who you are today. Be thankful for the successes you've enjoyed and even the mistakes you've made, because with a grateful heart any lingering bitterness fades away until only the beautiful memories and valuable life lessons remain.

Example: When's It My Turn?

Laura had so much going for her. She graduated from high school as valedictorian and was offered full scholarships to several top universities. It was tough for her to choose; so many colleges vied for her. Finally she picked one and was happy with her decision.

Her college academic record was as impressive as her high school accomplishments had been. She managed straight A's in all of her classes, even in the hardest courses meant to "weed out" students who weren't cut out for the program. Laura took part in exciting internships and represented her college in scientific competitions. By the time she had her master's degree in biomedical engineering, she also had seven excellent job offers. Once again, it was hard for her to choose, simply because all of them were outstanding opportunities.

Many fellow engineers, both male and female, were envious of her beautiful mind and the ease with which she seemed to grasp complicated material. How could anyone be so smart? And seven job offers? Some of her peers were lucky to get any offer after college. Laura, on the other hand, got to pick from the best of the best.

What they didn't see was that despite her amazing academic success, she wasn't satisfied with her life. In the same way that others envied her, she envied others. She felt that other women were prettier, more charming, and most of all, luckier in love. Laura had had a few boyfriends in the past, but the men ended up leaving. They were all married now, but she was still single. Her sisters were married. Her best friend was now getting married, and she was asked to be the maid of honor.

Instead of being happy for her ex-boyfriends, her sisters, and her best friend, she was too busy feeling sorry for herself. Instead of enjoying the weddings she was attending and being flattered for being chosen as the maid of honor, she felt resentful that she was "alone."

As a result, everything in her life suffered. Her promising career faltered. Guys she dated didn't call back, deflected by her negativity. Even her friends began to distance themselves from her, finding conversations with her to be downright depressing. Only her closest friends stuck with her and tried to help her out.

While several offered advice meant to help her get the man of her dreams, a couple of astute friends decided on a different approach. They decided that before she could be happy with anyone else, Laura needed to be happy with herself. She needed to adopt an attitude of gratitude for all that she had.

These friends started out by gently pointing out the many great things going on in her life. When this subtle approach didn't work, they tried a more direct approach. They told her that her negativity was sabotaging her happiness and driving people away. At the same time they assured her that they'd never leave her, and they told her they were willing to help her.

First they had her write a list of all the good things in her life. She could think of only a few things. But prompted by her determined friends, Laura came up with a few more items and then a few more. Finally, she had completely filled two pages with everything that was going well for her. She was amazed. She had never before stopped to count her blessings.

Next her friends had her give thanks for every item on her list. They asked her to give thanks for one thing on her list each day. Most days she remembered to do this. Little by little, her attitude started to change. She began to see how richly blessed she truly was. She also began to see how she was sabotaging her own happiness.

As her attitude started to improve her life got better. First her professional life progressed by leaps and bounds. She was given more responsibility at work, which eventually led to her leading an exciting new project. Then her life with her friends and family improved—she was very close to her parents and siblings, another blessing. Finally, things picked up for her in the romance department.

She started to date a nice guy, a friend of a friend. Three years later, they were married. By shifting her attitude to one of gratitude, Laura was able to turn her life around and eventually get her desired turn in love and marriage.

The Law At Work In Your Life

Have you met people like Laura, people who are perfect in practically every way but who sabotage their happiness by focusing on the one thing that isn't going right in their lives? Have you behaved this way at some point in your life? Are you perhaps missing good things right now simply because you choose instead to pay more attention to that which you don't have?

I have news for you: You will not get any closer to getting what you want by desperately obsessing over it. To get that which you desire but do not have, you must first be grateful for what you do have. In this way, you take the pressure off yourself. You can relax.

You already are successful—list and count the ways. You already have many blessings—again, make a list. When you see just how much you have going for yourself, you'll be enlightened.

The Law of Gratitude says:

Always be grateful for the blessings we have each day. Live your life with an attitude of gratitude.

You will get more when the universe sees that you are taking good care of what you already have. If you can't appreciate what you presently have, will you appreciate new gifts that come your way? Well, probably not.

By adopting an attitude of gratitude, you create a receptive aura or energy field around yourself. You maintain a calm demeanor. You don't get yourself worked up over what you don't have, because you're grateful for what you do have. You trust that by applying universal laws, you will eventually get your heart's desire. You don't stress over it, you don't obsess over it, and you never despair. You are at peace, knowing that everything happens at just the right moment.

To get more in tune with the Law of Gratitude, try the following steps with your child:

1 **Write down all your blessings.** It's been suggested to you before, now sit down and actually do it. Take a good,

close look at your life. Look at how many good things are happening for you right now. For one thing, you're alive! As long as you're alive, you have hope, and with hope, anything is possible. You child will often have no problem with knowing in their heart what they are grateful for. Many will even surprise you with the simple things they are grateful for. One child I know said he was grateful that his cat never got sick on him, only his sister!

2 **Now you and your child take the time to read back your list.** Spend a few moments thinking about each item. Next add at least ten more reasons that you're thankful.

3 **Once your list is complete, take out another sheet of paper.** For each item you wrote down on your list, write a note of thanks. For example, you may write something like, "Thank you for this place I call home." Or perhaps, "Thank you for delicious, nutritious food each day." Make it simple so that it stays fun for your child.

4 **You and your child should get up each day and thank the universe for three things you are grateful for in your life.** When you go to bed at night say thanks for one thing that happened in your day that made you smile.

5 **Gauge your positivity and your negativity.** Every time that you feel negative about not having something in your life, consciously counter that thought by thinking about something positive and feeling grateful for it. Teach your child to do the same. You and your child can even gauge this in each other. For instance one of my friends little girls told her father that when he came home from work he had no joy. Could he wait to kiss her until after he petted the dog - he seemed to be happier then.

6 **You and your child should learn to give thanks wherever you go.** You may do so silently. Before a meal, give thanks. At the end of the day, give thanks. When you're walking in a beautiful nature setting, give thanks. When you're with someone whose company you enjoy, give thanks.

Keep practicing being grateful. In this way, you will be more aware and more appreciative of all the marvelous things that you have. The more grateful you are for what you already have, the more you create an energy field of gratitude around you. Good things will then be attracted to your energy and come your way.

Affirmations To Use

You can give thanks for what you have at any time. You don't even need a reason to stop and give thanks—do it "just because!" A grateful heart is thankful for everything across the spectrum, from large blessings to small gifts to the simplest of pleasures. To help you practice developing an attitude of gratitude, try these affirmations.

> **Affirmation 1:** I give thanks this moment because I am grateful for everything—the big blessings, the smaller blessings, and everything in between. It's all good, and I am truly grateful.

> **Affirmation 2:** Everything that comes my way serves a purpose. Each experience is a learning experience, and an opportunity to grow in some way—spiritually, emotionally, mentally, in confidence, in grace, or in one of many other remarkable ways.

> **Affirmation 3:** Because I am alive, I am grateful. Because I take a breath, I give thanks. Because I have air to breathe and water to drink, I am thankful. Because I

have someone to call my friend, I am blessed. Truly, I am blessed beyond measure, and I am grateful.

Affirmation 4: Thank you for the trees. Thank you for the clouds. Thank you for the flowers. Thank you for the breeze. Thank you for the laughter of children. Thank you for the kindness of strangers. Thank you for all gifts, big and small. Thank you for everything.

Childs Affirmation: I am thankful for my wonderful life.

When you say affirmations that reflect how grateful you are for the countless blessings in your life, go ahead and get specific. Truly, there are countless blessings in your life, even if you are currently going through struggles and difficulties. It's just a matter of looking carefully. You will find them. Why not list them, and thank God for each one individually?

Exercises To Try with your child

Ever know someone who just seems lucky? They always win at bingo. They find $5 bills on the sidewalk. They win raffles. They seem charmed somehow. It's very possible—highly likely, even— that these people aren't extra lucky, they're just extra grateful. They appreciate what comes their way. They're not jealous of what others have. They're secure in themselves and content with their lives. You can say that they therefore create their luck by living daily with an attitude of gratitude. The following exercises will help you and your child develop this attitude as well.

1 **Create A Gratitude Ritual.** Walk through your home, from one room to the next, and give thanks for everything in that room. Give thanks for the water that comes out of the sink. For conveniences we take for granted. For the appliances in your kitchen that serve you well. For the décor that gives your place its own character. Each night before you tuck your child in bed ask them to

164

tell you one thing that happened during the day that they are thankful for.

When you and your child are enjoying yourself in the great outdoors, give thanks for the mountains, the ocean, the rivers, the trees, whatever natural beauty you encounter that fills your soul with awe. Ask your child what beautiful things in nature their hearts feel thankful for. Then ask them why.

2 **Call Someone To Say Thank You.** Did anyone do something really nice for you recently? Or perhaps even within the past year? Call that person to say thank you. Thank the newspaper carrier. Thank your doctor. Thank your child's teacher. The sole purpose of the call is to thank the other person, nothing else. Teach your child to say thank you for gifts they receive. Want to do something really fun? Write thank you on your bills as you pay them After all, bills are blessings for gifts you have already received. It's the gift of a home to live in, and even a car to drive. Looking at bills this way it is a much better way to look at them don't you think?

3 **Write A Poem.** You and your child need to put your gratitude into a creative poem. You can make it rhyming or not, whichever you prefer. The main thing is to get in what you're thankful for, and why. You and your child might want to write a short poem at the same time and then read it to each other.

Summing It Up

An attitude of gratitude can change your perception for the better.

Adopting a mindset and heart set of being grateful can make us more pleasant, calmer people.

An attitude of gratitude reminds us of our cosmic connection to all there is.

Being genuinely grateful is good for your body, mind, and soul.

There is tremendous power in gratitude—power to change, power to heal, power to turn your life around and get the most out of each day.

Be grateful for what you have now as well as for what you've enjoyed in the past.

By adopting an attitude of gratitude, you create a receptive aura or energy field around yourself.

The more grateful you are for what you already have, the more you create an energy field of gratitude around you.

Chapter
Eleven

The Law Of
Persistence and Results

"Wake at dawn with a winged heart
And give thanks for another day of loving."
— Kahlil Gibran

Chapter 10

In their book Dream It Do It: Inspiring Stories of Dreams Come True, authors Sharon Cook and Graciela Sholander name ten personal qualities they found in every dream achiever they studied, from Harrison Ford to Maya Angelou to Gloria Estefan to Lance Armstrong. One of these qualities is persistence. Here's what the authors say about the importance of being persistent when striving towards a goal:

> *"Perhaps life's rewards seem to escape so many because our society has forgotten how to wait. Expecting immediate gratification, we give up too soon, aborting the process prematurely and sabotaging any chance of success. Learning persistence is key to staying with our dreams long enough to enjoy results.*
>
> *As we follow our dreams we traverse new territory, and we can't expect immediate success while we grapple with the unfamiliar. Barbara Walters had to keep persisting to land interviews with leading political figures, a daunting and intimidating task. Barbara just kept at it and, over time, her exclusive interviews became her trademark and her ticket to her dream job.*
>
> *Most people who are recognized for their remarkable accomplishments started out stumbling and struggling just like anyone else. Each time we try, we learn something new that we can use next time. In the process, we build a reserve of knowledge that serves us along the road to reaching our dream. Each new attempt becomes a little easier, and brings us closer and closer to achieving our goal until we finally succeed."*

(excerpt from Dream It Do It: Inspiring Stories Of Dreams Come True, by Sharon Cook and Graciela Sholander)

Do you notice the direct connection between persistence and results? This is what the eleventh Universal Law is about:

The Law Of Persistence and Results: A winner never quits, and a quitter never wins. Hang tough and keep going. Persistence ultimately leads to results.

There truly is a direct correlation between being persistent and getting results. Too many people just give up on their goals because they don't stick with it long enough. How many times have you seen somebody give a half-hearted effort and then give up? Ask your child if they know of someone they thought might have given up.

What a shame, had they kept going, they would have achieved results, and this success would have propelled them to the next level. By giving up, though, they never even left the starting point.

You have to keep trying to get anywhere. This doesn't necessarily mean that you just keep repeating what you've always been doing. There comes a time when you have to try a different approach, a new tactic. This is effective persistence, and this is how people become successful.

What Does This Mean For You?

The word persistence has many synonyms, including perseverance, tenacity, determination, firmness, resoluteness, resolve, doggedness, and endurance. There certainly is a theme here, and that theme is: "Don't give up." You and your child should imagine that you have a personal trainer. Every time you feel that you're not making progress fast enough, or that it's too hard to get where you're going, your trainer appears and gives you a firm pep talk. He tells you, in a most encouraging manner, "You can do it. Don't give up now! Keep going." This is what persistence does for you.

Looking throughout history, it's the persistent people who ultimately achieve, as these examples illustrate:

- Persistence led Jonas Salk to develop an effective vaccine against polio. He began his work in 1938 searching for an influenza vaccine. Around 1947, he began to apply what he'd learned all those years to fight against the polio virus. By 1955, two million children had received the vaccine he'd developed against polio—they were the "Polio Pioneers." Prior to that, Jonas had tested the vaccine on himself, his family, and his laboratory staff. Had he given up at any point between 1938 and 1955, would we have a cure for polio today?

- Known as the "first woman doctor," Elizabeth Blackwell was the first woman to graduate from medical school and officially practice medicine in the United States. She applied to 29 medical schools and was rejected by every one. Elizabeth was finally accepted into Geneva College, a smaller school, but she was not taken very seriously at first. Fellow students, all male, made fun of her, and she wasn't even allowed to watch classroom medical demonstrations. She persisted. In time, she won the respect of her championed women's medicine and preventive medicine.

- Anne Sullivan was a young teacher who'd struggled with her eyesight her whole life. She had contracted an eye disease and went through many operations to try to improve her limited sight. Perhaps it was fitting, in light of her struggles that she would be assigned the job of trying to teach young Helen Keller. Through her loving persistence, Anne was able to get through to Helen and open up a whole new world to the child who could neither see nor hear. Thanks to Anne's persistence, Helen was able to first learn to communicate with the outside world, and later inspire us all with her wisdom and keen insights.

- Neil Armstrong became the first man to walk on the moon. He needed a lot of persistence to reach this incredible milestone. In fact he'd lived his whole life with dedication and persistence. As a young man he earned his Eagle Scout, the highest rank that a Boy Scout can earn. He then obtained a bachelor's degree in aeronautical engineering, and later a master's degree in the same field. He served in the Navy, where he did flight training. He became a test pilot. He served in the Korean War. He became an astronaut with NASA and went through rigorous training. Clearly, becoming an astronaut doesn't happen overnight. It's a lifetime of hard work and persistence.

Can you think of other persistent dream achievers? Here's a list to get you started: golfer Tiger Woods. Actor Jackie Chan. Ellen Ochoa, the first Hispanic woman in space. Louis Braille, inventor of the Braille system of reading and writing for the blind. Aviator Amelia Earhart. Clara Barton, founder of the American Red Cross. Pianist and composer Fryderyk Chopin. Go ahead and add some of your favorite dream achievers, historical and otherwise, to the list.

All these people have one thing in common—they kept going. They didn't give up their dreams when the going got tough. They continued forward, finding creative ways to overcome obstacles and keep after their dreams.

Each of us can learn much by observing how people reach their life's ambition. They get there because they keep trying. This is my advice to you. Continue to try. Approach it from a different angle, if needed. Try another way. But keep going. If you really want to reach your goal, don't give up.

Example: Learning To Ski

Ever since he was five years old, Paresh wanted to learn to ski. His parents were very protective of him, and they didn't know how to ski themselves, so they felt it was not in their son's best interest to take him up to the slopes and teach him. They felt his desire to ski was a phase he would soon outgrow.

Instead they supplied him with opportunities to learn many other wonderful things as he grew older. They bought him a guitar and paid for guitar lessons. Paresh's father taught him to play chess. They enrolled him in swimming lessons and art class. He was a busy kid, and he became a busy teenager. In school he did very well, and he was involved in many clubs and other extracurricular activities.

Still, that dream of learning how to ski never left him. So at the age of 21, even though he was now living on his own and far away from any mountains, Paresh decided to take a trip to Colorado for the sole purpose of learning to ski.

When he went out on the slopes, he was elated. He could not believe that his dream was coming true. After all these years, he was going to learn to ski. His initial lessons went well. He was encouraged by how quickly he was picking everything up. But when he got on the chairlift, he felt petrified. Being so high up distracted him, and he lost his focus. When it was time to get off the lift, he fell and couldn't get back up. He needed assistance; otherwise he'd get hit by the skiers behind him getting off the chairlift.

The rest of the day didn't go very well. He couldn't get his knees to bend enough to get him to turn properly. He crashed into others, or he fell on his bottom on purpose just to avoid crashing into people and trees. By the end of the day, his legs were killing him. It was such a relief to get those ski boots off.

Back at the lodge, Paresh was having serious misgivings. What had he gotten himself into? Why did he think skiing would be so great? Maybe he should cut his losses short and go home before he really hurt himself—or hurt his pride more.

But the next morning, he had a change of heart. After a good night's sleep he was ready to try again. He had remembered that deep desire he had as a child and as a teenager to feel what it's like to glide gracefully down the slopes. He was willing to try again.

That second day went a little better, but not much. He wasn't as afraid on the chairlift. He was starting to get the hang of turns. He could get off the chairlift half the time now without falling down. Even though his feet and legs still ached immensely at the end of the day, and he had a long, long way to go before he was even close to being graceful on skis, he could tell that he had improved, and this encouraged him. He spent some time in the hot tub to tend to his sore muscles.

The following morning, Paresh was more determined than ever. He had come this far. One more day of lessons, and he'd be done. He went in with a completely open mind. He figured this could be his last lesson ever, or he could decide to continue. He decided he wasn't going to have preconceived notions; he'd do his best and not think about anything beyond the lesson at hand. His job, he told himself, was to focus completely on what his instructor told him to do.

His persistence and determination worked well for him. During that third lesson, he advanced greatly. He went from being the worst student in the group to one of the best. He could get off the chairlift without falling. He could go down the slope without falling or without crashing into anybody. Speed and grace would come in time, he told himself. For now, he was mastering the basics, and he was proud of his accomplishments.

The following month, he decided to take another ski trip. After more lessons, he made major progress. The next year he came back to the slopes. And the following year, too. Soon he was zipping down faster than any of his friends. In another year, he joined an amateur competition. Paresh came in second place. His persistence paid off.

The Law At Work In Your Life

You know, we've all given up trying at some point. This is not necessarily bad. There are times when we need to give up because it's not what we're supposed to be working on. Stopping one endeavor enables us to look around and find another endeavor that actually suits us better. So please don't expect yourself to keep trying at everything, since there are times when giving up truly are in your best interest. You as a parent must teach your children when it time to let go and do this. Without making them feel as a failure.

However, most of us have given up too soon in certain scenarios. Had we kept going just a little further, we would have reached a goal. Or had we chosen to keep trying and persisted, even if it took us years, we'd be at a different place at this point in time. Perhaps we'd be more fit, or doing work that we really enjoyed, or making a difference in our community through a volunteer effort.

You need to distinguish between when you should keep going, and when you should stop. You have every right to throw in the towel. Just be sure you don't do so too early. Be sure you've given it your best effort.

Here is the Law of Persistence and Results stated once more:

A winner never quits, and a quitter never wins. Hang tough and keep going. Persistence ultimately leads to results.

175

Being persistent means being ambitious. It means keeping your eye on the prize as you continue to move forward. It means not letting every little bump in the road cause you to lose your nerve and end your journey.

To let the Law of Persistence and Results work for you, try these steps as a family.

1 Practice persistence. Are there any tasks around the house or at work that you've been thinking of doing, but you've been putting off? Do they require extra effort on your part? It's time to build your persistence. Choose one of these tasks to do.

2 Once you have chosen the task, do what you need to do in order to get it done. If it requires extra time, put in the necessary time. If it requires you to call someone and ask a few questions, do that. If you have to learn a new skill, do it. Continue working on the task, as you are able, until you are done. This teaches you persistence.

3 Make a list of accomplishments you'd like to reach. Keep your list to about four or five goals.

4 Next, look at your list and figure out what challenges you might encounter along the way. Write these down.

5 Now come up with possible ways to get around these obstacles. How would you resolve specific problems that might arise? Write these potential solutions down.

6 Choose one of the items you listed in Step 3, and begin working towards that goal. Use what you came up with in Steps 4 and 5 to continue moving forward with persistence.

One of the rewards of being persistent is enjoying the fruits of your labor. We're all human—we want results. When you are able to be persistent, you'll get results, the reward you're after.

Affirmations To Use

Any accomplishment takes time, and because so often we are tempted to give up along the way, persistence is an incredibly valuable quality to cultivate and to hang on to in our quest. These affirmations can assist you as a family learn how to embrace persistence and follow the Universal Law of Persistence and results.

Affirmation 1: I know that results don't happen overnight, but I also know that results happen. I will continue to work toward my goal, trusting in the law of persistence and results, which tells me that by continuing to move forward, I will attain my desired outcome.

Affirmation 2: Forward, forward I continue to march. Persistence sustains me when I feel weak and the road becomes blurry. Forward, forward I keep moving. Persistence ultimately leads me to results.

Affirmation 3: Everyone, without exception, had to persist to overcome obstacles. I am no exception. I will persist to overcome the obstacles in my path. I will continue to move toward my goal.

Affirmation 4: With persistence and time, I can do anything.

Childs Affirmation: I know, I will succeed.

When you keep trying, you'll get to your destination. Even though our society likes and expects instant gratification, you must understand that learning, growing, evolving, changing, and gaining new skills are processes. You can't learn to type overnight. You can't learn another language in a day. Everything that's worthwhile takes time and energy, and that's why persistence is such an important ally for you. Teach your child the mind set that a quitter never wins.

Exercises To Try With Your Child

Persistence leads to results. These exercises are designed to give you and your child the results as long as you are tenacious and determined. Try them. You'll grow in persistence, and you'll have a reward at the end, too.

1 **Build Or Make Something.** What you build or make depends on your particular skills and on how ambitious you want to be. Ask your child what skills they feel they have or want to have and as a family build something. Here are some ideas: Sew a dish towel. Build a three-dimensional puzzle. Bake a cake. Make a wooden napkin holder. Put together a photo album. Make a kite. Make a quilt. Build a fence. Even very young children have skills to offer, even if it's just licking the batter of the cake spoon.

The important thing is to have something tangible when you're done. Pick something that might take you just a little bit out of your familiarity range. Follow the steps carefully and meticulously. Take your time. Do a good job. When you're done, enjoy the rewards of your efforts. Why not ask your child if they would like to build something for someone you all love, like a grandparent? The bonus is the great feeling you will get in return for giving them the gift.

2 **Try It Again.** Is there something you've tried in the past but weren't able to succeed? Try it again. For example, have you tried to flip omelets or pancakes but couldn't get the hang of it? Try it again. Did you try roller skat-

ing but felt too wobbly? Try it again, this time on a nice, smooth surface (no ruts) and wearing knee pads, elbow pads, wrist guards, and a helmet. Go nice and slow until you can do it. Persistence pays. As a family not everyone is good at the same things, so help each other out when doing this exercise.

3 **Arrange Dominoes.** You've probably seen it done on TV; a person painstakingly arranges domino pieces in a row, or a spiral, or some other pattern, one next to the other. After every piece is in place, knock over the first domino. It sets a chain reaction that goes fast, knocking all the dominoes over in an exciting burst of energy. Your reward? The thrilling little show of your creation! Try to find bigger dominos for very young children to work with. Better yet, why not make them out of wood as a family project? When you do this exercise as a family, it will teach both you and your child a little bit about patience, but it's also sure to bring out the giggles in young children.

Summing It Up

There is a direct correlation between being persistent and getting results.

Too often, people give up on their goals because they don't stick with them long enough to enjoy results. Learn not to let yourself or child fall into this habit

Other words for persistence include perseverance, tenacity, determination, firmness, resoluteness, resolve, doggedness, and endurance.

To reach a goal or a dream, continue to try. Approach it from a different angle, if needed. Try another way.

Keep going. Don't give up, unless you feel you truly need to move on to another endeavor.

You need to distinguish between when you should keep going, and when you should stop.

Being persistent means keeping your eye on the prize as you continue to move forward with ambition and determination.

One of the rewards of being persistent is enjoying the fruits of your labor.

Chapter
Twelve

The Law Of
Service

*"How wonderful it is that nobody need wait a single moment
before starting to improve the world."*
— Anne Frank

Chapter 12

We are not here merely to serve our own needs. We're here for each other. When hurricanes strike, when emergencies happen, when a person needs consoling or uplifting, that's when we need each other the most. Serving others never goes out of style—it's here to stay, and we would do well to become experts in this arena.

The United States Peace Corps was established by executive order in 1961, and authorized by Congress later that year, with the goal of promoting world peace and friendship. Feasibility studies were done prior to the official launch of the Peace Corps, and Dr. Maurice Albertson was instrumental in crafting a study that considered the advisability and practicability of such a venture. His feasibility study created a model that became the very framework for the brand new Peace Corps.

Since its inception, the Peace Corps has grown by leaps and bounds. More than 187,000 Peace Corps Volunteers have served in 139 host countries, working on pressing issues to help humanity. The organization is recognized globally as a positive force that benefits communities everywhere. And Maurice has the satisfaction of knowing that he helped start this vital organization.

In a recent interview in Colorado, Maurice had this to say:

> *"We have to overcome the temptations of greed and make service as important as the profit motives. It's just that simple. And that's why we're here."*
>
> *– Maurice Albertson, KUNC-FM radio interview, Greeley, Colorado, 2/22/07)*

Service has been at the center of his work his whole life. It began at home, with him watching his father help others. With Maurice's engineering expertise and his genuine concern for the environment and the wellbeing of people everywhere, he's helped to develop programs that address the environment, water and sanitation, water resource development, on-farm water management, and other critical areas.

Now at the age of 88, he's still going strong. Collaborating with a group of retired Peace Corps volunteers, he's developing a plan to end global poverty. He calls this initiative Village Earth: The Consortium for Sustainable Village-Based Development. He shows us that service never ends, and that those who put the law of service into practice benefit personally from the purposeful, rewarding life they create.

Here is the twelfth Law:

The Universal Law of Service: We are an interconnected humanity. When we serve others, we also serve ourselves.

When we put others before us, and tend to their needs, our own problems start to fade. By putting others first, we empower them and ourselves. Serving others is what we are here to do. We help our fellow man, woman, and child. We also empower ourselves because we can only move forward, as individuals and as humanity, by remembering to turn around and give a hand to someone else. It does us absolutely no good whatsoever to advance and be "number one" if we've left others far behind. Now there is a big difference between enabling someone and empowering someone, and you yourself should be aware of the difference before you teach your child about the Universal Law of service. There is an old saying that states; buy a man a fish and he eats for a day, but teach him to fish and he eats for a lifetime. So when you become of service for someone, reach within your own heart to see if that statement rings true to you or not.

What Does This Mean For You?

There are many ways to serve others. As always, look at your set of skills, your talents, your gifts, and your interests. Look at where your passion lies. In this way, you will get a better picture of how best you can serve. Service comes in all forms: Sometimes it could even come in the form of writing a book that helps others, inventing a new medication to cure heart disease or even inventing a new software program that will benefit the world. Here are a few words that could describe being of service.

- *Teaching*
- *Healing*
- *Empathizing*
- *Building*
- *Contributing*
- *Uplifting*
- *Empowering*
- *Employing*
- *Inventing*
- *Calming*
- *Explaining*
- *Protecting*
- *Helping*

You can serve through work, at home, or in a volunteer capacity. You can serve spontaneously. If you see someone struggling in some way, step in and help. No need to wait to be called upon. Opportunities to serve abound. Use a motto many others have applied: Think globally, and then act locally. Teaching your child how to be of service as a family will be sure to instill in them the mind set to be of service when they become adults.

Example: Michael Helps

Michael was your typical teen. Did pretty well in school, loved sports, and was completely absorbed in video games and basketball. He was a good, quiet kid who stayed out of trouble and tried to be responsible.

One crisp fall afternoon, he was hanging out with friends at the basketball courts in the neighborhood park. They were just shooting hoops, enjoying being outdoors in the fresh air, laughing together, having fun. He had just taken a shot at the basket when, out of the corner of his eye, Michael noticed something that didn't look right.

The person in the wheelchair was far away, so he couldn't quite tell what was happening. All he saw was the chair going back and forth, back and forth along a stretch of walking path. What's going on? He wondered to himself.

His friends called him so he got back to shooting hoops with them. But he kept looking over to see what, and how, the person in the wheelchair was doing. Nothing had changed—the chair just kept going back and forth.

"Hey, guys, I gotta check this out. I'll be right back," Michael suddenly said. He ran full speed to the person. When he got there, he noticed it was a woman, about his grandmother's age. He cleared his throat and politely asked her if he could be of service.

She looked up, surprised to see someone there as she hadn't noticed anybody coming by. She'd been so absorbed in what she was doing. "I can't seem to get around this part of the path," she said. Michael took a look. The section she was trying to get through was full of twigs, leftovers from a broken tree branch.

"Let me help you," he said. First he brushed the assortment of twigs to the side. Then in a flash, he got behind the lady and carefully pushed her through. "There you go, ma'am."

With a big smile on her face, the woman thanked him profusely. "No problem," said Michael, and seeing that she was on her way, he went back to shooting hoops with his friends.

When my own daughter Jennifer was only about twelve years old she had to have foot surgery on her left foot and had to use crutches when walking. One day she wanted to go see her brother Jeffrey in a play he was in at school. Normally this would be no problem, but we lived in the state of Michigan at the time and we had three feet of snow on the ground. Lo and behold Jennifer lost her footing, fell, and broke her other foot needing now to trade in her crutches for a wheel chair. What we discovered as a family was not only how to help Jennifer get around in stores, and on icy sidewalks, but it helped us as a family also to realize how important it is to be of service to help other people in wheel chairs.

The Law At Work In Your Life

There is no shortage of opportunities to serve. Every one of us can be of service in a million different ways. You and your child just need to figure out how to plug in to serve. Do you like books? Libraries often seek volunteers. Love animals? The humane shelter could use volunteers to help care for the animals there. Many children love to be of service in this fashion. Maybe you and your child can visit a local nursing home as many older people living there never even get visitors.

You can also be of service through work. For example, forest rangers serve by protecting our forests. Teachers serve by teaching and guiding the next generation. Police officers serve by keeping our communities safe. Computer technicians serve by repairing computers we rely on. Accountants serve a business and all of its employees by keeping the financial end of the business in good order. You have the opportunity to serve whether at work or off work. A good way to help your child understand about being of service through work is to let them talk to a police officer, teacher, or even forest ranger and ask them why they serve in this fashion. Who knows it might even strike a spark in your child to choose this as their own career when they grow up.

Look at the Law once more:

We are an interconnected humanity. When we serve others, we also serve ourselves.

How would you and your child be serving yourself by serving others? In addition to feeling useful and getting a real sense of satisfaction, you'd be helping to create the kind of world you want your own child to live in. The kind of world in where all people have their basic needs met. A world where everyone has the opportunity to live the life they are happy with.

You and your child will also get the satisfaction of knowing that you are helping to create a world that's more equitable. No, you can't help everyone, and you can't fix huge problems all at once. But with everybody doing their part and being of service in some way, we can make a significant dent on those problems. We can all keep whittling away until the problem's gone. And even those issues that remain will be easier for people to handle, because of the compassionate service that you and your child are putting into it.

You and your child can start to master the Law of Service through the following:

1 Look around. The need is out there. First figure out what needs exists in your community.

2 Once you've analyzed the situation, take an inventory of you and your child's skills, abilities, and availability. And then ask your child where he or she might think there is a need. Children often have different ideas then adults do.

3 Also check your heart and your passion. What causes are you and your child passionate about? Where would you like to make a positive difference?

4 Now that you've done your homework, plug in somewhere. Join a cause you both believe in. Help someone, somewhere. It could be visiting people at a nursing home. Helping someone by pet sitting while they are away. Collecting returnable bottles and donating the money, even helping someone plant flowers. There are many, many, many needs.

5 If you get tired of working on one cause, move on to another. But be sure to apply your abilities towards helping someone, somewhere. You and your child are a valuable resource. You both can make a difference.

6 In addition to being part of a cause, serve on a spontaneous basis. Like Michael in our earlier example, step up to the plate when you see someone who needs assistance. Teaching children to help in this way is always a plus for the world.

There will be a time when you or your child will need someone to help you. Today you serve someone. Tomorrow someone serves you. In some ways, the Universal Law of Service resembles the Law of Giving and Receiving. When everyone does his or her part in service to others, the entire world is united in a network that watches out for each other and makes sure needs are taken care of.

Affirmations To Use

It is tremendously rewarding to be of service to another human being, or to a member of the animal or plant kingdom, or to our planet in general. When you watch the news, for example, what are the scenes and stories that touch your heart the most?

- *The person who reaches across cultural and racial lines to help someone in need*

- *The firefighter who rescues the family pet*

- *The dog who saves its person friend from a catastrophe*

- *The students who help an underprivileged family in their community*

- *The "good Samaritan" who risks his or her life to save another's life*

Service does the heart good. Try it—you'll like it! You might even get hooked on it because it feels so good. As you serve others, hold these affirmations about the twelfth Law, the Universal Law of Service, close to you.

Affirmation 1: To serve is a privilege. By serving others, I create good will that comes back to me.

Affirmation 2: I serve with a cheerful heart. For in serving others, I get so much more in return. I am grateful for the opportunity to serve.

Affirmation 3: Opportunities to serve abound. I am but one, but I am, and I can. By choosing to serve others, I make a difference.

Affirmation 4: We are ONE. When I serve you, I serve myself. Service to others is service to self.

Childs Affirmation: Because I live, I give.

In service to others, you affirm your ability to make a difference. You affirm your ability to make ours a better world. You affirm the worth of your fellow human being, as well as your own worth as a caring individual.

Exercises To Try With Your Child

When you and your child get into the routine of being of service, it's easy to do. You can be of service whether you're an introvert or an extrovert, whether you prefer being around others or being alone. That's because there are literally thousands of ways to be of service to others. I even save receipts from a local grocery store that will give a certain percent of what I buy back to charities of my choice. When I buy Fresh Step Kitty litter for my cats they have a program called Paw Points that I can donate to an animal charity www.mypawpoints.com . So you don't even have to leave your house to be of service to others and the world if you don't wish to. How easy is that? Let these exercises get you started on ideas. Then, you and your child can master mind and think up your own ways to be of service to others.

1 **Volunteer With an Organization.** We've already mentioned some possibilities before. Through Habitat for Humanity you can help build a house for a family that is experiencing financial challenges. Through the Red Cross or the Red Crescent, you can help in areas where natural disasters strike. They will train you, too.

What organizations in your community work to help others? Call them up and find out what volunteer opportunities they have available. Then choose one group you'd like to work with. Many animal shelters accept help and this is a great way to let children who love animals be able to enjoy their company. Who knows your child may be a Vet or even a zoo keeper someday. Let your child learn how to do fund raisers or help you in the fund raiser you are involved with.

2 Visit Local Homes for the Elderly. Many times these places have opportunities for you and your child to be of service. Many older people never get visitors. You could call the homes for the elderly in your area and see what ways you and your child can be of service. Maybe just having a visit with the elderly people would be a great way to be of service.

Or better yet why not have your child draw a picture, or take flowers from your yard to people there. What a great way to bring a smile to the hearts of older people who may be lonely. I have known many children who enjoy the stories that these older people have to share with them.

3 Look For Opportunities, and Fill In. Don't wait to be asked. Who in your neighborhood could use some help? Is there a single parent who could use your baby-sitting services? Someone leaving town that might need pets cared for or plants watered? This is a great way to be of service and help your child learn about responsibility at the same time. Being of service does not mean you can't accept money for what you do, if THEY offer it. If someone offers your child money for doing the yard work, shoveling snow or walking their dog for them, allow them to accept it. It will be a way for you to use the opportunity to teach your child entrepreneurial skills when this happens. Someone who needs a ride to work? Needs exist in your own town where you may be of service. Help clean up the trash in the area where you live. Organize friends to help clean up a park or stream. Many areas have nature centers where you and your child can take part in nurturing the animals there. I held a seminar in Michigan once at a nature center called the Howell Nature Center. I called the center and asked them for a list of what the center needed, and gave it out to everyone coming to take my seminar. Cost of the seminar was donating something on the list. You should have seen the entire wonderful things the parents and children donated. They donated bird food, cracked corn, newspapers; one family made bird houses, and then together placed them in the forest. What a great way to be of service to Mother Nature don't you think?

Summing It Up

We're here for each other.

Serving others never goes out of style—it's here to stay, and we would do well to become experts in this arena.

Those who put the Law of Service into practice benefit personally from the purposeful, rewarding life they create.

Opportunities to serve abound. Think globally, and then act locally. You can help your community and you can help people halfway around the world by acting locally.

Every one of us can be of service in a million different ways.

Figure out how to plug in to serve. Ask your child for ideas of ways they think they could serve others.

By being of service, you help create the kind of world you want to live in.

In service to others, you and your child affirm the worth of your fellow human being, as well as your own worth as a caring individual.

Carrie Carter has taught thousands of people "The Secret" to unlocking their intuitive side to Manifest their greatest desires.

At the age of five, Carrie became aware of her intense intuitive gifts and connections to the Universe. These gifts have given her an amazing ability to help others overcome their personal fears and live a more balanced, peaceful, and abundant lifestyle.

Through her workshops, personal coaching, and writing, Carrie shares The Universal Laws of Abundance to shift the way people think and change their habits to help them get rid of the blocks, heal past pain, move through grief, and attract the abundance in their lives that they have always desired.

Carrie has made numerous appearances on ABC Channel 7 with the Kelly and Company Morning Show. She has also been interviewed on FOX News Channel 12, Drive Time Talk show, Houston News Radio FM97.5, BBC Radio network in London, UK; CBS network Radio in Washington DC, and Inner Vision KPFK radio in Los Angeles. Carrie was featured on ABC Channel 7 News, and she has been published in numerous news articles which include; the LA Times, San Antonio Express-News, Denver Post, Woman's World Magazine, and Detroit Business Review.

Her on-line course, "Think Your Way to Riches Family Style" is the preeminent resource to discover "Hidden Keys" that unlock the twelve Universal Laws of Success for parents and their children. She has recently produced visualization and meditation CD's which help unlock the success consciousness for all who listen.

Her third Book, Think Your Way to Riches Kids' Style, is a synthesis of Napoleon Hill's Great Classic, Think and Grow Rich, which she turned into a "workbook" for parents who want their children to be successful in all areas of their lives.

Carrie's passion is to help people on their inner journey to discover their personal road map for abundance, peace, and happiness. Her main passion is to give children worldwide the "Tools" which are lacking in the normal educational system and understanding to create the abundant lifestyle of which they are all worthy of. Experience Carrie's educational seminars, workshops, and private life coaching.

For more information or to arrange an interview with Carrie Carter call 810.714.3338

Printed in the United States
200273BV00003BA/142-198/A